T0157105

Ants into Butterflies
Becoming Comfortable
Being Uncomfortable

Xavier "Mr. Hope" Robertson

BALBOA.PRESS
A DIVISION OF HAY HOUSE

Balboa Press books may be ordered through booksellers or by contacting:

Balboa Press
A Division of Hay House
1663 Liberty Drive
Bloomington, IN 47403
www.balboapress.com
1 (877) 407-4847

Because of the dynamic nature of the Internet, any web addresses or links contained in this book may have changed since publication and may no longer be valid. The views expressed in this work are solely those of the author and do not necessarily reflect the views of the publisher, and the publisher hereby disclaims any responsibility for them.

The author of this book does not dispense medical advice or prescribe the use of any technique as a form of treatment for physical, emotional, or medical problems without the advice of a physician, either directly or indirectly. The intent of the author is only to offer information of a general nature to help you in your quest for emotional and spiritual well-being. In the event you use any of the information in this book for yourself, which is your constitutional right, the author and the publisher assume no responsibility for your actions.

Any people depicted in stock imagery provided by Getty Images are models, and such images are being used for illustrative purposes only.
Certain stock imagery © Getty Images.

Interior Image Credit: (Chapter Art and Chapter 4 "W-hand))- Diamond Symone; (Chapter 2 "Squirrel Boy" John Singleton Copley, Museum of Fine Arts

Print information available on the last page.

ISBN: 978-1-9822-4451-4 (sc)
ISBN: 978-1-9822-4452-1 (e)

Balboa Press rev. date: 03/09/2020

Contents

Prologue

There comes a time in your life when you'll realize that you are gifted with the knowledge and direction of being exactly what you are designed for, or you're gifted with the realization that you absolutely have no idea about it! Both realities result in the same circumstance that whatever it may be, it surely will not occur today. So how does one endure this period of uncomfortability? How can one maximize today with enough fulfillment to make prosperous actions that lead toward the reality of a desired future to minimize the lows, defeat procrastination, attract wealth and success, and thus become what you're meant to be? Ants into Butterflies...

This journey is certainly not full of hand-me-outs and surely not for the faint of heart. You may have or will soon realize that the outward battle is easy to subdue but to overcome the battle within, one must continuously conquer to emerge victorious. The uncontrolled thought patterns, irrational reasoning, "wasting" of time and overall analysis paralysis or stagnancy must rightly be in check. Reality is perspectives after all...does an Ant evolve into a Butterfly?

Becoming comfortable being uncomfortable is not to desire to make our current circumstances more bearable. Our desires and goals are of our future realities; being and existing within that which we are destined and designed for. The fruition of these realities is enabled by allowing that which is causing discomfort to become the fuel for this transformation whilst maximizing where you are today! Be the Ant now and flourish as the Butterfly you are destined to be.

CHAPTER 1

Find the Ugly

Find the Ugly

L ike many of us, in my early 20's, I thought the world and society sucked. This feelings crept into me because I felt that the reason why I wasn't where I wanted to be even with the right "credentials" was because everything was outside of me and out of reach! I had zero amount of ownership or accountability. Life has a plethora of nuisances and with the added irritant particulars of my own life, one could easily discover my distinct detest for the current state of the world. I could easily describe my dissatisfaction with politics, equality versus equity, discrimination, poverty, world hunger and on and on. Trust me, I have more in store! Thank God I was able to realize that everything I felt that could be used to improve the world were all the things about me! Yes, me! Yes, down with Xavier! Blame me for the indigestible volumes of racism. Yes, blame me for the developing countries that are still without adequate water supplies in the 21st century! But none of those things are the issues of MY world. I was shouldering issues from everyone else's unique world, and not just my own.

Now, does this discredit or deduce my emotions and my thoughts to these issues? No! I was applying too much of my energy on the things that I'm not in the current position to adequately effect a change on. Also, I am deficient in this aspect since I am without the right tools and lack the right approach with what I can offer (as of now) to have the necessary change that's needed. Once again, because these things are not readily the issues of my world, it doesn't deduce my passion for these issues. Many of these, I believe I can and will still facilitate the change needed, and also the changes the world's needs as well. But displaced energy is so detrimental to you, to those around you and to the world at large. When you are not using or operating in the gifts you were sent to utilize to achieve that very purpose, you become a cancer to your reality, to those around you and the world. You become a vacuum, sucking up all positivity and creativity around you. But being a vacuum in this instance isn't an entitlement or a platform for you to find arrogance or comfort as you are sucking up the very resources needed for anything around you to manifest at its highest capability! When your gifts are actively utilized and are in sync with the correct thought patterns and energy being focalized, the seed you sowed becomes able to prosper.

Energy and Matter are the only two confirmed elements in the universe; it is believed that only the Creator possesses the power to turn these two elements into living beings. We have been given this same power through our thoughts. Like the soil, whether it's carrots, poison, or flowers that are planted in it, if watered, the soil will render the fruition of whatever seed is planted! This is precisely the same with our mind. How we use positive energy flow, creativity and thus exercise these into actions, then are we gifted with the fruition of desired realities! But, let's not get ahead of ourselves. We will dive into the power of mind just a little later. First, let's continue to structure our self for this capacity.

So yes, when you are not operating correctly in what it is you are meant for, you hinder everything you touch or those around you from prospering or reaching their potentials. Now, the critics will argue "I'm not affected by anyone else's shortcomings or lack of realization of who they are," but the thing is, you do become hindered from the possible sprouts of euphoria that your energy and another could have had or were even "meant" to experience!

Now, does that mean that someone else or thing won't fill that void? Surely so, but how many times have we wished to have a certain personality in place of another, not in a negative connotation of who the universe has privileged you to experience, but it's about YOU! Do not allow the world to miss out on greatness because you couldn't get out of the way of your OWN self.

As Mr. Dwayne Carter would put it "On the road to riches, it's just a little traffic." What I realized as I started passing through some of these trucks and cars is that the individuals driving the cars, "the traffic," "the people in my way," and "the MAN holding me down" was that, "the traffic" was just different versions of myself...Yes, different "me's." These weren't the good "me's." No, you're not reading a comic, but Superman does save the day! That Superman was the version of me that realized that these versions (the traffic) of me were toxic to my progression.

- The "Late but I'm great X"; late to easy things and still deliver greatness, but people tend to remember the time wasted a little more than the message or the service delivered.

- The version of me that couldn't let a $2 dollar Tuesday pass by, a Friday night out with boys (really Mon-Sun), taking Saturday's just to "chill" or the Sunday unproductive "Me Day." This Version has many faces, but this _____ (fill in the blank with a version of you that fits this) "me"!

- I was the procrastinator but could still bust an "A" on an exam, test, or assignment, God!! Though procrastination just meant I delayed the opportunity of creating greatness in those moments as well as the opportunity to progress that greatness into something better. I missed being opportune with even more ingeniousness for an A, a good job done or a great service that could've been complemented; complemented with a new invention, a start liner to a best-selling book, or intuition to make a call or move that could have greatly impacted your future. But, our favorite lie to ourselves always happens to be, "My best work is always when I wait," and this prompts our time to be filled with pointless-rendering activities, which could have been time spent judiciously sprouting even more achievements.

- The X that was always defensive and on guard and not as "receptive" as I thought I was. The X who was also the hearer but listened and retained nothing. The X that was eager to be felt and heard but deaf to the feelings and the sounds sent back, not knowing when to speak and listen.

- The X that was inconsistent with sticking to and staying on course with the process, the diet, the workout plan, studying, staying with good habits and quitting the bad, taking the extra mile.

- The X that had to realize he reaped everything he sowed and that you literally reap everything you sow! This X or version is another _____ (fill in the blank).

I can go on and on, but I want you to take a few lines or pages and write out all the good and bad versions of yourself and use what is best for your future. I have provided two blank pages here for you to do so. Pause, did I just insinuate that some "bad" versions should stay? Yes, because "bad" and "good" are relative terms. A prime example is prohibition. It was "bad to be caught with alcohol at one point, but now showing up to any event without party favors is the easiest way to never get invited to a party again! So, that "bad" version of yourself may have been operating in the wrong environment or at the wrong time and just needed to be applied differently or for situational purposes only. After you apply this process, carefully watch how your world begins to maneuver differently about you. I had to release these toxic versions of myself so I could progress further and further through the traffic.

What's interesting about this highway is the fact that it is never ending, which in the real sense isn't annoying or tiresome but quite interesting because older versions arise differently with new forms and new situations. This often arises just as you always have weaknesses or areas you can always strengthen. What's interesting is that you'll have the desire to remain constantly alert to explore these areas of weakness, thereby permitting you to progress into success faster and more adequately! The traffic starts to dissipate in twos and threes and you get to "enjoy the view" or enjoy the time in your reality that you have created for yourself; the slow times, the times of relaxation and reflection etc. Find the ugly! Find every version that has caused ill/negative outcomes in your life. Find all the versions of you that won't be present in a future version of yourself that you desire. Find the YOU's you don't like and become the YOU you have always envisioned and desired to be!

NOTE

NOTE

CHAPTER 2

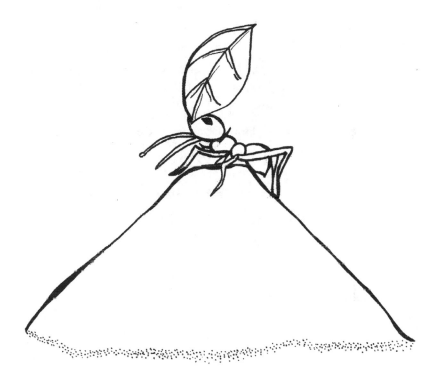

Be an ant now

Be an ant now

How to maximize the now when you're beauty is meant for tomorrow

This is by far one of the most strenuous tasks to master. This is one of the many reasons I chose this ideology to be so early in the book; "Tackle the big ugly frogs." This will by far be the most grueling period of your life. For some, it won't take long to get the idea while for others, they might have to kick it a little longer. I like to think of this period as "The Bed of Stones: Getting Comfortable being Uncomfortable." It is the realization of your calling, your greater potential or discovering what you're designed to do. However you frame it, it is a beautiful and an amazing experience. Sadly, it is shared with one thing, and that is "Time." Oh, how we hear it over and over and over; right place wrong time! This lucid element is so intangible and non-manipulative, so we have thought. Yes, I am implying that time can be controlled and to our favor. What's interesting about Time is that we are teased with the desire to know tomorrow, but in Time's arrogant gloat of secrecy, it leaves us with information of value in the past. Today and yesterday and the day before, all share in value and information, enabling control and the ability to yet predict the future. So, where's does this tie into you? When realizing your innate godly abilities, you are immediately humbled with the realization of the lack of necessary resources and circumstance to execute your greatness. Or, you are without that greater source of inspiration or hindrances in your life rather it's emotional, verbal or physical abuse; further prohibit the expression of your power and purpose. You realize that you are not in the right place or that you lack the right quantity because your appearance and deliverance doesn't match the product or service. So what's next? You know you're great or meant for greatness and a few others too. How do we then endure the Now?

Lesson one: Patience. Pack your patience because you're in for one thrill of a ride! This is the first step in manipulating and thus controlling time. Understanding the WHEN is an essential factor here. So many things prosper and others dwindle in the noise of society because of anxiousness and lack of the ability to foresee when something is most impactful. Comprehend that phenomenon as well accepting that often your desires will not transpire in the "instantaneous now."

"A Boy with a Flying Squirrel," by John Singleton Copley (1965). Museum of Fine Arts, Boston.

"It took me 9 minutes to notice that the shape of the boy's ear precisely echoes that of the ruff along the squirrel's belly —and that Copley was making some kind of connection between the animal and the human body and the sensory capacities. It took about 21 minutes before I registered the fact that the fingers holding the chain were exactly the span of the diameter of the water glass beneath them. It took a good 45 minutes before I realized that the seemingly random folds and wrinkles in the background curtain are actually perfect copies of the shapes of the boy's ear and eye."

I love this analogy by Dr. Jennifer L Roberts, who taught on "The Power of Patience." This precisely describes the phenomenon of "Fruition is Time." It's wasn't until she gave it enough time that she reaped the full benefits of the understanding! How many success rendering opportunities or riches have you misjudged for that of "squiggly lines?" Golden opportunities, golden-ships (friendships, network-ships, business-ships, etc.), golden moves, golden achievements, and on and on. All because we didn't allow the right time to come to manifestation or give adequate time to something so as to bring it to materialization. Time can be described in five words: You Do or You Don't! This unfolds the lucrative pockets of time! For some, this gave them instant hope and reassurance, and for others here's the explanation. Understanding how to maximize the best You in every season is the key to bringing your desired reality to fruition. This is where we pull from the past and stay still in the moment. What do you wish you would have done? To help guide you on this reflection and journey, this will serve as a guide and manual you will put into use to help orchestrate your future. I will explain my own reflection, but I want you to think of yourself within these reflections and pull the renderings from your unique reality.

I realized that in order to adequately shape and thus control my future, I had to reflect on my complete past, and I took an in-depth look on all the events. The first place I started with reflecting into my past was a very familiar place; my parents (this is another fill in the blank as this figure or figures should be a person(s) that hold great influence to you; an older or authoritative figure(s))_____. On this specific reflection, I focused on all the lessons I had listened to and the ones I wish I coulda,' woulda,' but didn't listen to or follow. For example, since I was little, my dad told me I needed to read more and my mom kept telling me to write more as well. Whew, I was pretty a bright child; always did well in school and in other areas too. My parents knew I was intelligent, but in my arrogance of knowledge, I read what I wanted and when I wanted. On my transformation into being better (the Glow Up), I embodied the importance of reading and writing daily, and boy, I was grateful for finally embracing a lesson I took so lightly and long to realize. But, what I really took for granted was the fact that they reached into their past to a place where they had hoped they had done more and applied it to my reality to positively affect my future! This example is to serve as a purpose that we all have some form of an authoritative or person of influence who we value that has a plethora of wisdom that can greatly affect the reality of our futures. If you don't have this figure or mentor, then it is necessary to get one because it is one of the first things you must have on your path to greatness. There's no better teacher than an individual who has lived through challenges and wants to be an open book to help you pick and choose from situations and stories to adequately apply them to your world so as to make you a better being.

PBnJ: The World's Greatest Sandwich! Whether you agree or not is still the greatest. The PBnJ's are key takeaways from various topics discussed as we journey from Ants into Butterflies

~ (PBnJ) Power of a Great Mentor

A great mentor is one of the greatest assets you can have on your journey to success. There's no greater influencer or combination than an individual that has lived what you haven't, desires to be an open book and also desires to see you succeed farther than them. If you're lucky (humbled and focused), you will have multiple of them as well as some who will choose you! These are my 5 qualities of a great Mentor and what you should look out for before becoming someone's' Mentee:

1. "Mentors are free"

If anyone is requiring you to pay to gain knowledge from them, then know that they only desire to make you as good as what you can afford.

Mentors are free, which is why who they are and what they can provide are invaluable. Offering payment because you desire a certain individual since it is one of the limited ways you able to get yourself in a room with them isn't a bad thing either. The true Mentors will love the tenacity and either decline the payment or make it based upon what you will produce from the mentorship and challenge the compensation to be an end goal.

2. **"Mentors desire to mature you both personally and professionally."**

A great Mentor understands the balance of personal and professional life and desires to make sure you're attending to both adequately. They are able to identify weak areas that you cannot see for yourself and will challenge you to become a better person.

3. **"A Mentor reestablishes your hope and will not bite their tongue to professionally tell you to "get your shit together."**

Some tend to just go with the "get your shit together." A great Mentor will be able to identify when you are not acting or operating within your highest capacity and challenge you to immediately get back on track. They will do so in a way that gives hope and reestablish your confidence. They will provide methods, tools, readings, programs and etc.to equip you with the ability to regain focus and not slip in such a way moving forward. For those who need to hear this now…GET YOUR SHIT TOGETHER :).

4. **"A Mentor is a great source of network."**

A mentor should be able to facilitate viable networking opportunities. A great Mentor, when they cannot deliver knows someone who can assist them to open doors that they cannot unlock. On matters they do not have expertise in, they link you with someone who will steer you in the correct direction of where you can gain the needed assistance.

5. "Mentors are transparent."

A great mentor desires not to show all of their accolades but all their flaws and shortcomings as well. A great Mentor does this so you can have a true depiction of success. This helps you to be enabled to repeat where they excelled and avoid where they failed.

The next aspect of my past I tuned into was what others used to say about me (both good and bad). This is a very impactful reflection. I tuned into that of which was bad first; this is because these reflections are two-fold. Listening to what was bad depicts two things: It enabled me to take the present into observation to see if those same things were still relevant. It's also gave me the exact negative items and the qualities/habits I needed keep away. Reflecting upon the good gave me the idea to see how I positively affected the world around me. What did others enjoy about my company? What did I add to my different environments? This peer reflection should be filtered through true friends, family, employers, teachers, etc. This reflection will give you a tangible measurement to whether you are positively positioning yourself for the future you so desire. This is where the importance of having true company lies.

(PBnJ) Keep the squares out of the circle! It is imperative for the future you so much desire that you to choose your circle carefully. I'll say this in a few ways: (1) associating with different minded/focused individuals will divert you from your goals. (2) vibing with the wrong energies will drain yours as well (3) true friends challenge the process of an idea, and not the idea itself (4) your circle should have a challenging presence of betterment, not keeping one another down or stagnant, so one can "catch up" (5) the wrong individuals close to you can be the very cancer to your dreams. Your circle should elevate you and not the other way round. Your close associates (friends, homies, girls, bros, besties, partners, team mates, etc.) should

- Have like-mindedness of overall wellness of the entirety of the group.
- Have like-mindedness of desired successful future.
- Challenge you to be the best version of you at all times.
- Challenge you to evolve into being better
- Promotes and praise your good qualities and also give constructive criticism to areas you could improve on.
- You all are conscious of how you complement each other's lives and maximize that very aspect and divert to nothing else.

#Squad

Another area I tapped back into was "whose life did I impact? How was I still impacting them as well as whom was I impacting now?" This gave me a clear image of whom I was and whom I had become. I reflected on when I came in contact with individuals both from the past and present, and the perception of me that they had experienced. This measurement of perception is not to be confused with likability. Anything beyond an understanding of where one stands in the lives of those particular individuals is out of the realm of perception. This understanding of perception as stated before gave me a clear measurement of who I actually was then and whom I have grown to become now. Now, that I have these two individuals (me), I'm only missing one, the future me! So with this understanding of what was and what is, I can ultimately create what is to be. I started in familiar places. I started with self-reflection, identifying differences in appearance; the way I spoke, even how I dressed, my approach to others and overall approach to life and what my priorities or focuses were then vs. now. The more I dug into this area and reality, it continued to break down into smaller more unique vantage points that served as tools for me to reconstruct myself to be rendered.

(PBnJ) Social Perception.

How were you and how are you currently being socially perceived? This is a good measurement of who you think you are and what others actually view you as. This helps one avoid a plethora of misconceptions, unwarranted situations, gives insights on what to do and a clear understanding of where you stand within your reality. For many, we think we have attained these roles or are on track to become a particular piece to a puzzle. Whether this ideology of a role attained is within someone's life, within a business or within life itself, we are shocked by the outcome of where we thought we stood does not match our reality. Now, one would either stop here or tune into what is truly happening around them. In the midst of "jealousy and hate" (criticism) and the realization of where you stand, we find these beautiful jewels for advancement. It's only partly true that "what others say does not matter," as constructive criticism or "people just hating," whatever is fitting for you, provides a clear indication of where you are. Social perception is a great tool but oftentimes, many get caught in what is being said or done (and not done) and fail to realize the benefit of what has happened. This is not to be mistaken for taking on everything others say, as they may not be true or applicable. The world has a way letting you know very abrasively whether you're on track or not; if only you allow yourself to be in tune with the right avenues of inspiration and influence. Adhering to these notions correctly and tuned into the right avenues of inspiration and influence allots for advancement rather than destruction. So, let's look at the enormous amount of negative social perception experienced by one particular group for a very long time. This particular group is still fighting to be equal in the eyes of their opposite. Social perception, if used properly becomes a map on how to guide oneself from ant to butterfly. This particular group is 'Women.' For centuries, they have been deemed inadequate both intellectually and physically to that of men. This social perception discouraged millions from their true potential, but for many more millions, this gave them a direct understanding of where "they are not" and where they had to go (purpose). In a nutshell, people will always have something to say (social perception) and if you only listen to the words, prepare to be lost forever. But break down what is being said and if any inkling has any application to you, they have just given you a free insight on where you can become better! Women were told they weren't enough, but now they are attaining more degrees and intellectual milestones than men in today's society. Women were told that they didn't possess the emotional stability and tenacity to be leaders, but currently, there are more women CEOs than ever before and high level corporate businesses worldwide are being dominated and controlled by Women. #LeaveTheEmotionsAtTheDoor; AKA thick skin; "Please, tell me everything you think I am or could be so that I can become all that I am!"

NOTE

NOTE

CHAPTER 3

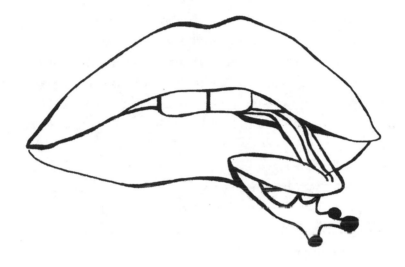

Eat That Frog

Eat That Frog

Yes, you read it right! Now, no we aren't going to be literally eating frogs even though frog legs have been compared to that of chicken legs. So, what does eating frogs have to do with success? Now before I continue any further, I must give complete credit to Brian Tracy who wrote the book, "Eat That Frog." The remainder of this chapter will give a brief summary of the book 'Eat That Frog' intertwined with its applications to our journey from ants to butterflies. I highly encourage and recommend that you read the book for your future's sake, and learn how get out of your own way to affect that change you have always wanted. One of the easiest ways we get in our own way is procrastination! Brian Tracy has beautifully described this phenomenon. See, I was the "wait the night before to do an assignment/paper/hw/study and still get an A" King! But how foolish I was! We'll leave that there, and let's reflect on some great takeaways Mr. Tracy has gifted us with. Eat that frog is composed of 21 essential ways we can stop procrastinating, eliminating enemy numeral Uno, OURSELVES. Let's take a little time to briefly describe each of them as Brian introduces us first to the "Three D's"…

1. Set The Table

"Clarity is perhaps the most important concept in personal productivity. The number one reason why some people get more work done faster is because they are absolutely clear about their goals and objectives, and they don't deviate from them…"- Brian Tracy

You have to be absolutely clear about what you want. Take a step back to when you were a kid in preschool or kindergarten. The teacher asked you a very simple yet powerful question. At 5 years old and only having been able to comprehend this world for only about 2-3, you didn't hesitate and you were elaborate. This question was "What do you want to be when you grow up?" Oh, how we marveled at this thrilling question! I want to be a firefighter, I want to be the

President, or a Doctor, A Football player, and for some, specifics came. "I want to be a Marine Biologist, I want to be a Nurse for babies" and etc. Then the teacher with even less hesitation asked why. "I want to be a doctor to help sick people," "I want to be a police officer to protect others," "I want to work with animals so everything and everybody is happy," got to love our youthful selves. But what is interesting as the years go on and we are faced with this question in our late teens, twenties or when we meet that crosshair in the road, our reply becomes "I don't know" (adds shoulder shrugs) or we go on to state what someone has told us to do or to follow. "Well, my dad said I should…" "Or my aunt thinks I should follow after my…" then we ask why and few have definite reasons that revolve around our image of "financial security." So, I challenge you to channel your inner youth. What do you want to be when you grow up and why? Take a second before continuing to read on and actually write this out with detail!

When we were young our thoughts were not thorough, but they were enough that they made sense and laid the foundation for our dreams. Now that we're older, we have to create this same clarity.

PBnJ –

1. Decide exactly what you want.
2. Write it down.
3. Set a deadline on your goal; set sub-deadlines if necessary.
4. Make a list of everything you can think of that you are going to have to do to achieve your goal.
5. Organize the list into a plan.
6. Take action on your plan immediately.
7. Resolve to do something every single day that moves you toward your major goal.

"Clear written goals have a wonderful effect on your thinking. They motivate you and galvanize you into action…."- Brian Tracy

2. Plan Every Day in Advance.

As Homo sapiens, we are gifted with self-awareness. In that self-awareness is the reflection of where we are now and our desires of where we want to be. Properly mixed together with focus and clarity; we just learned from step one that we must have foresight. Our ability to think and plan is one of the most powerful tools known to man! Maximize you peace, your focus, your happiness, your time, your money, etc by planning ahead!

3. SIX P FORMULA.

"proper prior planning prevents poor performance"- Brian Tracy

We have heard this phrased with a few different "P" words used, but all lead to the same destination. As humans, we make life so big at times, and we are neglectful of the fact that life is very simple. Few people practice planning even day-to-day because they feel they must make every minute count or become overwhelmed with what should be placed in the right position. This is because as we learned from step one, clarity was absent. "Planning is simple, all you need is a piece of paper and pen."

PBnJ—

Start with very simple tasks and consistently achievable actions. We are always striving for quality over quantity. Don't begin with trying to plan every minute of your day. Start by setting a wake up time and bedtime, plan your breakfast, lunch, dinner, (1) 15-30 minute productive time slot, and (1) 15-30 minute leisure time slot. Begin to adhere strictly to this very diligently and increase gradually adding or lengthening productive time alone and balancing your life with that of leisure time. Start every project with a list. Organize each step by priority and synchronize it to flow and be consistent with the overall goal. Place the list in multiple places so that you will see it throughout the day. Complete each task one by one. Even though some tasks might be inter-correlated, try to isolate each and every one; being diligent in completing each task to its fullest degree.

4. 80/20 Rule TO EVERYTHING.

"20 percent of your Activities will account for 80 percent of your results"- Brian Tracy

This means 20 percent of your products or services will account for 80% of your profits. Literally, apply this phenomenon to everything! 20 percent of what you do everyday accounts for 80 percent of your resulting future. What does your 20 percent consist of? Life is simple, so if we fully apply this phenomenon to every facet of our daily lives, we literally are controlling 80 percent of our future! Depending on how successful you truly desire to be will be determined by how far you dig into each 80/20 within your products, services, success habitats and etc. You will find that the "80/20 rule exist within each 80/20 and within that 80/20 another 80/20 and so on"- Richard Koch. 80% of your profits come from 20% of your consumers and 20% of those consumers are truly responsible for 80% of the 20% that drives the 80% of your profits. Embed this phenomenon into your daily actions.

PBnJ

Number of Tasks versus Importance of Tasks

Let's take for example you have ten tasks. Each of the ten tasks may take the same amount of time to accomplish. But one or two of those tasks will contribute five to ten times more value than any of the others. This is individualized so you have to identify these "heavy hitters" in reference to said goal as it could be one action that contributes 90% of the desired success or two to three. Apply this phenomenon to your schedule, routine, individualized goals and reconstruct the order of your tasks, time spent and overall approach until you have full proof consistency that continually elicits desired results that are time sensitive. As time is relative, but it is always of the essence. The wealthy and highly successful, all have a consistent formula that they apply across their businesses, schedules, and etc that allows them to consistently create the fruitions they so desire. Find your "Heavy Hitters" and maximize from there!

5.   Consider the Consequences.

The number one reason for failure is overestimating and underestimating the chances of something going wrong. This is because we do not properly analyze our actions. What makes people more successful than others is their ability to think and create what will be in 5, 10, and 20 years. How? No, they aren't fortune tellers, maybe, but I sure wish it was that easy. But they properly analyze what they did in the past that has now yielded their current results/realities. Today is the result of what you did yesterday. One more time, 'Today is the direct result of what you did, yesterday,' the day before that and so on. Today will become you tomorrow's yesterday. Literally, what you do today will be produced tomorrow. Analyze what are the most impactful, meaningful, success rendering, actions you can make strategically each day that will begin to render and form the tomorrow you so desire. We must analyze where others have also taken this path and study where they succeeded and failed in order to create a further detailed map that guides us quicker and with less mistakes to our desired realities. Many people fail because they fail to study the past, there is not much that hasn't been done, but much to be recreated and advanced upon. Don't go out trying to reinvent the wheel when you were meant to design a new way the wheel could function. Take the necessary time to study the industry you plan to thrive in, study those before you, and be focused where the pitfalls are so that you adequately avoid them or maximize them. This is embedded in maximizing the Law of polarity which we will discuss in just a few chapters.

6. Practice Creative Procrastination.

Wait a minute, isn't this whole thing about not procrastinating? Yes, but here's the thing, we all procrastinate. The idea here is to become a creature of habit and intent. "The difference between high performers and low performers is largely determined by what they choose to procrastinate on…" Paul Minors

Freebie- There is some things we can do less of that actually propels us further into our desired successes. We can do less drinking, less "turning up," less eating of unhealthy foods, less time wasting, less unorganized plans, less just going with the flow, less_____(fill in the blank) I want you to take a second before continuing to write out what in your life you could be doing less of, what is it hindering and what will happen when you begin doing less of the said thing. For example, if I do less drinking, when I work out it won't be counterintuitive, and I will see faster and better results that overall renders better (sleep, focus, completion of goals and more!

I can do less of:

7. ABCDE METHOD.

Let's take it back to Grade school by priority setting our entire task with the ABCD or E. A is of course the most important, and A-1 is more important than a-3. Without diligence, sticking to completing each task by priority (tackling the big ugly frogs first), and choosing to complete the easiest tasks just for gratification (the tadpoles) is the exact determinant and reason as to why your success will never unfold to the degree of your liking or if at all. Don't start eating at A-4 or B-3 until there isn't a scrap left with A-1!

8. Focus on Key Result Areas.

Key result areas are defined as areas that are within your complete control. These are the areas of actions and habits that will generate consistency and that will lead you toward your desired future. Many of these key result rendering actions will be of intrapersonal habits. We sometimes let success or the excitement of success to allow us to forget the "bread and butter." There are specific acts, habits, thought processes, mindsets, vibes, outlooks, approaches, and on, that are specific to the reality you wish to endure. In sports like basketball this would be like practicing 100 free throws every practice, or in baseball/softball taking cuts off the tee, or in dance practicing routine splits and turns, even as professionals! Everything has a process, a protocol, and formula to which and why it exists. This is the same for the future you desire or are designed for. Your variables will consist of actions, people, places, time and a plethora of other acting forces. The individuals whom are currently living the life you wish to live have allowed their formulas, processes, and protocols to become embedded into their DNA...The most successful people in life have become creatures of habits of their key result areas and attributes to why it comes off like their success is done effortlessly. This is because once you identify the formula to which continuously renders the outcome you desire, one must now only repeat and adapt it to move with the ever changing world.

PBnJ's

Ask yourself this question; *"What one skill, if I developed it in an excellent fashion, would have the greatest positive impact on my career or success...."* – Paul Minors

9. Apply the Law of three.

As we learned earlier, life is much simpler than we make of it. Statistics and Theory indicates that there are three essential core tasks that you perform consistently that are the centerfold of your reality. You subconsciously do these tasks every day. Your ability to identify these areas or not will set the aptitude and altitude of your success.

PBnJ

In thirty seconds, write down your three most important goals in life right now. Your subconscious mind will go into a form of "hyper drive" and your three most important goals should pop out onto the paper.

1. _____

2. _____

3. _____

Freebies-

1. Work all the time you work.

2. Balance isn't an option it's your life!

10. Prepare thoroughly before you begin.

The huge mistake often made which leads to procrastination or not completing the task is not having enough time gathering the correct tools. As we learned earlier from the "Six P Formula," failure to properly prepare only leads to further setbacks and hardships. Now, the thing is that we all are victims of common mistakes, and most of us ponder on this question. How do you know that you have prepared adequately or have gathered the correct tools to build the future you so desire? Listen! We must have an ever conscious ear to the world and our inner voice,

PBnJ—

In life, we meet "Push" and "Pull" doors. When we have goals in mind, we become ecstatic…Most of us know and embody the "Six P Formula" but still run into "setbacks." This phenomenon is tied directly into the quality of perseverance. We become even more excited when we have developed the much required clarity and its plan. So, we begin the journey toward this goal, "la-didi-la-la" with the assumption that all our effort just needs to be "pushed forward." Grind, grind, grind, and then we hit the "Pull Door" and were pushing. We push, push and push again. We re-evaluate our plan, check that we're in D-drive and press on even harder. Trying different angles and the door still won't budge! As we met "Push" doors, the work that was required seemed effortless, we had prepared adequately enough that the fruition of our reality required only correct time and focus. This "Push Door" ideology can be defined in many ways and is more comprehensible to what is required in order to advance; as we just have to push forward, than its counterpart, the "Pull Door." "Pull Doors" require you take

1. "Move back,"
2. "Step to the Side,"
3. "Pause," or
4. "Succumb to Foresight" in order to advance.

WHOA. See, to advance in life does not always transmute or require a physical forward motion. We often allow the ideology of "physical forward motion" to be falsely related to grinding or success rendering actions. Also "Treadmill" mentality. For example, "age" is often regarded as a supreme notation of wisdom or expertise on a subject; we know this to not be true.

The lack of ability to recognize, and/or understanding what to do when faced with "Pull Doors" will either cause more procrastination or prohibit the completion of the said goal. What do I need or need to do in order to get my desired goal? What is prohibiting or where have I lacked that has placed me at a "pause"? The first step in maximizing on "Pull Doors" is recognition. Why is this "Pull Door" requiring us to move back, take a step to the side, or requiring me to pause and succumb to foresight.

The "Pull Door" requiring the Move Back

Sometimes, when we get into the mode of success, we have our heads down and we're just attempting to grind away. Like a flower requiring both light and dark moments, our dreams and reality require from us to pull back and allow what has developed to breathe. Social media and the ever go-go society has created this demand for immediate results, immediate validation, immediate success, adoration etc. We think that if things do not happen immediately or within our self-made time frame, then they weren't meant to be. Oh, how many grand and wealth rendering ideas have been vacuumed up by this way of thinking! We have become afraid of allowing things to breathe and organically grow. Are you okay with tomorrow? What if I told you that your job today was all foundation building and seed planting? What if I told you that you had to eat scraps for 5 years in order to have a lifetime of gourmet foods? The reason we cannot apply what needs to be done to our dreams and move back is because integrity tells the tale that we are not consistent with what is required. Are you reading and becoming ever knowledgeable of what it is you're striving to be great in. The world changes daily and one should be knowledgeable of the time frames or factors that require a change, in regards to your goals, in order for them to be still be in line to come to fruition! This "move back" could also require additional schooling, going back to get certifications, licenses, becoming credentialed etc. This "move back" when faced with a "Pull Door" is recognizing that there are essential resources, tools or habitual actions needed in order to advance.

The "Pull Door" requiring the Step To The Side

"Pull Doors" could require us to "step to the side." This is the evaluation of current positioning, your surroundings, and if this is the most opportune place for you to grow and prosper. Often, we thrive

31

to press on and grind on with our dreams without evaluating if this is the right building, the right event, the right job, the right city, the right state, the right region, the right country etc. We often feel confined to where we grew up because that is all we know. It's comfortable and makes much sense to start from where you came from right? So many dreams have diminished and have been swallowed up because of individuals being too afraid to leave home and start elsewhere. I challenge you, what's holding you back? Family? Friends? Money? The Fear of survival? Fear, Fear, fear? Fear or False Evidence Appearing Real. Allowing your mind to transmute irrationalities into physical forms. The world is like a book and where you are born or where you were raised is merely but a few pages or a few chapters in an ever written interminable book. We have restricted and cheated ourselves from so many euphoric possibilities and opportunities. Traveling is not only of human nature, but it's also an absolute necessity in ones journey to developing and creating the future that one desires. The interaction with the unique architectures of the earth in various areas of the world, renders euphoric exhilarating creative experiences. Do not allow the comfort of your home to prohibit you from the comfort of a desired reality. Do not allow family, friends, and other alike ties to confine you to an area you were not meant to grow. If you were an architect would you stay in a place that already has the buildings they desire? Palm trees do not prosper in the desert.

The Pull Door requiring you to Succumb to Foresight

Alike the pull door requiring the move back, this door requires you to move back so that you foresee everything it is you're about to endure. With push doors we can find ourselves in interesting situations. This is not because we are without the tools needed to prosper in our endeavors, but it weighs on the true capacity of our preparation and we sometimes do not land exactly where we planned to. This pull door is a special commodity, as we are not always gifted with this strategic pause. This door is also one that you can create for yourself. We can create this door long before we even start as well in the midst of the process while working toward a goal. Being able to foresee a plethora of possible outcomes of your plan will be one of your greatest assets. This is again shared in the habit of being completely knowledgeable of the "field" or "arena" of your dream. I like to think of this door as the "Miss The Hype" door! Again the Universe does not give everyone the privilege of this strategic pause, instead it is only for those who have harnessed resilience and have decided upon a worthy trade off of services/products for a desired reality. This pause is the Universe saying "I have not placed you here to get content or to get complacent, do not allow the hype of comfortability, familiarity of people and places and the quick reaping of a derivative of your desired reality to outweigh the true goal." Sometimes, we get in a season where we are close to or on track to reap the said goal/dream and we allow ourselves to become comfortable with doing just enough to reap what we think is an acceptable amount of our desired reality. We become entertained by this reality, but we must press for the true euphoric experience that's rooted in being just a little more disciplined, just a little more focused; but we got time right because we can turn it on at any moment, right? Nah! This is the most entrapping, setback rendering, and dream destroying mindset. Time is always of the essence and one must possess an ever going resilience toward advancement and growth. Appreciate and cherish the moment when you realize that you are capable or could do more and then DO IT! Do that extra set, study that extra hour, stretch a little longer; GO!!!!

Push and Pull doors.

Take One Oil Barrel At A Time

If I told you that you had 3 minutes to eat 200 wings in order to win the grand prize. Most individuals' minds instantly run to "I have to eat 200 wings." This thinking will primarily lead to procrastination 9/10 times, if the task at all will be completed. When we are faced with that big ugly frog or that huge task, the trick is to not see the task in its totality. Instead, decide what are single actions that can be done leading to the completion of the task at hand? In light of our analogy my goal no longer becomes to eat 200 wings, but to focus on the wing I have in hand. You don't have to save the world in one day instead it should come one step at a time. Before you know it the wings are gone! Stop making Life bigger than it is and tact away at it perseveringly in smaller droves. The most successful people are able to dissect their challenges in smaller projects and are rewarded with accomplishing even more. Remember, life is simple, the greatest world advancing moments have been of simple actions, and the ideology that life is "big" is a mere distraction created by fear.

11. Upgrade Your Key Skills.

The only thing that is known to be consistent in this world is CHANGE. No day is like the last. With that in mind, in order to stay on top or to stay the best at what you do, you must continue to ever evolve into becoming better. One of the reasons we procrastinate is the lack of confidence to complete the task at the level that will render the exact desired outcome. The elites are ever conscious of "next;" either how to become it or benefit from it. With this level of consciousness, the elites are ever evolving themselves into better personalities consistently by looking to mature, grow, elevate, or increase their skills sets. What the most successful, and individuals alike living your desired reality all have in common is an ever longing to be ahead of the rest. The elites are ever reading, ever attending seminars and workshops, ever creating, and thinking! This hunger drives the successful to be extremely knowledgeable of their craft or profession, conscious of the need to evolve or adapt upon the shifts in standards of the world, and extremely focused on being the best positioned vessels to receive everything hoped for!

Pbnj

In order to get ahead you must STAY AHEAD.

Three steps to mastery

1. Study intently and extensively in your field, for at least one hour every day.
2. Become knowledgeable of how your craft or position affects the world, as well as how the world affects your craft or position. Understand what affects your desired reality negatively and makes it vulnerable of ceasing to exist.
3. Never settle. Never admit defeat. "It's not how you start, it is how you finish." Complacency and Contentment equal Death.

12. Leverage Your Special Talents.

We are all very unique in our own way.

Because you exist, you have specialties that no one else has, "There are certain things that you can do, or learn to do, that can make you extraordinarily valuable to yourself and to others," but it is up to you to identify this. What abilities are natural, second nature "could be done in your sleep?" You become exceptionally valuable and "expensive" once you realize what makes you special, you then discover how to maximize it. There comes the ability to market it, and to advertise that unique ability that is above that of others striving to do the same. Leverage is creativity. Thus, the ability to be exceptionally creative or possess the ability to create what is highly desirable amongst many is what creates the reality you desire. The rich have become rich because they render skills, talents, gifts, abilities that transmutes into things society can't exist without.

13. Identify Your Key Constraints.

Between today and where you want to be tomorrow, there is something in the way that is hindering its fruition. What is holding you back? What is negatively affecting the outcome of your actions? When you identify these constraints you are then gifted the ability to control those things thus controlling the rate at which you get to desired goals. We often are our own biggest constraints. So, I challenge your hunger to get to your said goals. We as well allow hindrances in our lives because of fear. We are afraid to end-ships (friend, business, relation, situation, and fill-in-the-blank_____) or end habits whilst knowing they beget only negativity or make us stagnant in our current or past realities. Do not allow today's gratification or validation to outweigh the greater degree of advancement you could have for your future self. What within you or within your environment have you allowed to become unaddressed barriers?

Great Barrier ME:

1. _____

2. _____

3. _____

4. _____

5. _____

6. _____

14. Put Pressure On Yourself.

"Only about 2 percent of people can work entirely without supervision. We call these people "leaders" Now, you must ask yourself if you are a leader or a follower. Followers need set schedules (set by others), someone to tell them when, what and how. A leader is able to place fire under his/her own butt and get going. If you have a goal in mind, it will always be you alone that can hinder its fruition. We can list all the societal restraints that prohibit us from reaching our desired goal, and how this could be better and if I was born with this and etc. All these things are outside of yourself; when you make everything intrapersonal and become the leader of your own life, you will then realize that no outside forces can hinder you from completing your goals. You must apply this type of pressure to yourself. This is rooted in integrity. Integrity is defined as what you do or who you are when no one is looking. Your parents can tell you to read more, and if you tell them you are and can make it seem as though you are, then they cease to bother you any longer. But when you are being faced with a test or an opportunity to advance and because you didn't study in secrecy, you then fail publicly. You have to develop a habit of applying strategic pressure on yourself. We all know that eating healthy foods and working out produces longer, healthier, wealthier lives, so why are you scarfing down fast food everyday thinking that it is not affecting your work ethic. Remember, all things are interconnected. This pressure can never ever come from the outside in, but only inside out. You have to truly want a better standard for yourself. "Due Diligence" = You ain't doing shit. Due diligence says go to school and if that didn't work at least you went. Or maybe you finished and was not able to land a job in the field of your choice, and in the desired time so now graduating was enough. In many ways, we all come across these moments where we are subject to quitting after fulfilling our rendition of what we believe our "due diligence" is. With the outcome equating to failure we now fail to move past it. Fate doesn't exist, and one of the biggest believed lies known to man that at some point it was meant to be this way. No, at some point you lost your creativity, your drive, closed your eyes to foresight, found complacency or didn't continue to allow yourself to ever evolve to be that version that renders your desired reality. Fate only becomes truth when we admit defeat. Time is relative and in its relativity it's always "Day one or One Day." We are gifted with the opportunity to ever evolve into what is expensive and essential to the world.

15. Maximize Your Personal Powers.

Briefly touched on this in #14, but maximizing your powers are rooted in self-care and self-awareness. "Your body is like a machine that uses food, water, and rest to generate energy that you then use to accomplish important tasks in your life and work. When you are fully rested, for example, you can get two times, three times, and five times as much done as when you are tired or burned out." Protect your energy! You should have daily routines that effectively garner your mental and physical health. Strategic breaks from life (working out, sports, recreations, etc.) Balance is not the key, it's your life! Health is wealth!

Pbnj—

Overworking can mean under producing

Work at your own pace

Get enough sleep

Guard your physical health

16. Motivate Yourself Into Action.

Our biggest battles are won and lost in our heads. You didn't make that move because you obviously psych yourself out. How we feel or go about life is the direct result of how we talk to ourselves. Daily self-affirmations are the keys to your well-being and building blocks of your desired future. "It is not what happens to you that matters, but the way that you interpret the things that are happening to you that determines how you feel. Your version of events largely determines whether these events motivate or demotivate you, whether they energize or de-energize you. To keep yourself motivated, you must resolve to become a complete optimist." You do not have to accept reality at face value. But your power to reshape what is happening to you allows you to maximize the situation with which to render the best outcome for your future self. Self-reflection; I was a server for a chain restaurant and other servers can attest that for the slightest mishaps customers would have your head. In their fury of having felt that they had been underserved or the food not being to their liking, we servers were the first to feel their wrath. Now, if I allowed myself to take on their energy and apply their disgust to how I thought of myself, or alter the task at hand, I could've ended up in unwarranted debacles or have lower self-esteem. But I allowed myself to perceive these high energy situations differently. I analyzed all that I did, where did I lack or where could I have had a higher level of concern. My internal voice took over, my affirmations flooded to the top of my thoughts and I became even more empowered to control the present and render an even higher self for the future. "You must refuse to let the unavoidable difficulties and setbacks of your daily life affect your mood or emotions."

17. Get Out Of The Technological Time Sinks.

A break from technology, social media, and the desire to feel ever connected, can and will save your life! Technological advances are at the highest they have ever been. Everyday a new app, or website, game, system, product, OS, or an improved efficient service is born and rooted in technology. While technology is great and is ever pressing the human race forward, it can be the most detrimental thing to your success. I'm not here to knock out social media by any means as it is the platform for most business, and the most elusive way to stay connected or to connect with anyone in the world. But too much of anything, even good, is dangerous. "Continuous contact is not essential; you have a choice!" Before Mark Zuckerberg thought of Facebook, we were still very well connecting with our family and friends. Before the era of social media, life was lived, the sky was still blue, and the sun still shined. In order to "check-up" on others it wasn't as easy as a swipe, more time was spent with tangible interactions, and real happiness existed rather than quick and false gratifying fixes from likes or hearts. I strongly challenge you to take a 30 day break from all social media. For those that require it for personal businesses, or your jobs, I ask you limit your social media interactions to only that of work for this period (no personal tweets, reposts, picture uploads, etc.). What would happen if at every traffic light I didn't have to check my phone, or I didn't spend my first minutes of awaking in bed surfing through pointless feeds, or if I didn't have to capture every moment on social media to make it "real or authentic"?

Here is what would happen:

You will be happier and more content with life…

In the virtual reality of social media, it's very easy to compare your life with your colleagues and belittle yourself. While we will argue that it's a source of motivation seeing others attain that which you wish to have one day for yourself; further research shows that depression and anxiety are higher because you're chasing perceptions. Social media elites can shape their lives through post and pictures whilst in reality, they are not even those people. It is highly unlikely that anyone is going to put their bad moments on display for all to see. If someone travels around the world on holidays, there will probably be a picture of it on social media, but if their landlord just kicked them out for not paying rent, they probably won't mention it online.

You will be more productive…

Social media is quite entrapping. What was meant for a quick status update turns into 30-40 minutes of scrolling. A habit done 30 minutes a day can result in high proficiency in just a few weeks to a few months. What if you spent 30 minutes on a language app, or piano lessons, or reading within your field, or dream-rendering activity instead of reading that Samantha had the best latte ever today (for her 3rd time this week) or Keith posing in his Challenger that's been #newwhip for two weeks? At work, you can get a lot done instead of peeping on your phone every now and then. It can be very easy to deceive yourself by trying to limit your social media use, but how many times has a planned 15 minutes on social media turned into 2 hours? You don't fight temptation, you avoid it.

You will be grateful for your life…

Instead of being envious, jealous or desiring someone else happiness, you should find happiness in your own. There are more than 7 billion humans inhabiting the world today; if you have food, clothing, and a roof over your head you are richer than 75% of the world! If you woke up today 1 million plus didn't make it to see this week. Some of us are wishing to be adored in the comments like people we follow, while 500 million people live in starvation and wish to have a consistent meal. This is where social media can create depression. We chase after irrelevancies of life. But when we log out of social media and log into life we discover just how privileged we are to even care about "only getting 37 likes."

Your relationships with others will improve...

Social media has made so many people more insensitive to others and has altered how we interact with others in real life. We can talk for so many days on a chat, then meet in person and it all becomes silent. Social media is causing more and more people to lack substance. How many interactions have suffered because we cannot disconnect from our phones. We are the most connected generation this world has ever seen, but we are further apart than any other generation in history. "Seeing" friends and family everyday has resulted in not actually seeing friends and family again all because of the social media flair. Texting and chat apps are destroying more and more relationships because they are emotionless with the plethora of emojis because everybody interprets certain things how they want to. If you were having more conversations in person more relationships would still be intact, and overall a greater respect for the others would exist.

You will see how beautiful the world is...

The world in which we live in is such a beautiful place and we think we are seeing how beautiful it is through a screen. False! We should be striving to experience real life around us and traveling often. "I'm here for a good time not a long time"-Drake. We aren't on earth a very long time and yet we are being limited by social media.

You'll be innovative…

Being on social media for too long makes you less creative and less innovative. Being constantly distracted prohibits your mind from wandering to more creative thoughts. Social media drastically affects our emotions which thus, influence motivation and creativity at all levels.

What you do today ultimately affects your future. So, taking breaks from social media benefits you in these ways and more. This will result in more happiness and attribute to more success. I challenge you to take a 30 day break from all social media and watch how your productivity and overall mood toward life improve. As exclaimed above, technology and particularly social media isn't the only culprit to our mal interactions. Our actions determine what we are rendered. The algorithms on these social sites are designed to reflect what we and our "friends, followers, etc." all choose to interact with. This being said, what you're exposed to is the direct result of whom you follow and vice versa. So, as we touched on earlier, whom we choose to befriend or associate with affects our futures. Following fitness oriented individuals will result to you being exposed to aspects that reflect that category. Choosing to follow individuals that fabricate unrealistic lifestyles will result in desires that are also unrealistic to your current reality and to where you are trying to go.

18. Slice and Dice the task.

How do you eat steak? Let's all picture that we have a steak in front of us. Before you eat the steak what do you grab? A fork and a knife? Correct. Then does the steak begin to magically appear in their mouth? No, you cut a portion of the steak to eat it and continue to cut and eat the steak until it's all gone. This is how we must do with our task. We must slice away at it on a daily, weekly, monthly basis and whatever it takes in diligence until the goal is met. If we try to do too much at once we get less done, become overwhelmed, counterproductive and risk not meeting the goals we set at all. Rome wasn't built overnight, there is no such thing as an overnight success, and quick gratifying successes only lead to more setbacks. It's a marathon not a race. Set your own pace, we need a sense of urgency but attacking a goal too wholesomely could be very detrimental to the desired outcome.

19. Create Large Chunks Of Time

Highly important task requires more time or for time to be used very particularly.

Pbnj

1. Schedule blocks of time.

2. Use a time incremented planner.

3. Make every minute count.

In relation to our Slice and Dice method, time management will aid in maximizing the time that's needed to prepare and execute said goals. Mark Twain said, "The secret of getting ahead is getting started. The secret of getting started is breaking your complex overwhelming tasks into manageable tasks, and then starting on the first one." *Like your money, time is also scarce. It should be spent in accordance with the goals and dreams that you value the most. If you spend your time wisely, you'll achieve an amazing state of fulfillment, where not only are you achieving your outcomes, but you're also satisfied with your life and your role within it. "Time is that quality of nature which keeps events from happening all at once. Lately it doesn't seem to be working."* — Anonymous.

Chunking simply means grouping together information into manageable chunks, so you can use them to effectively achieve the outcome you desire without stress. Write out all of your task, Identify which are related (Money, Family, etc) and prioritize their importance based upon desired future outcomes. Tony Robbins method on executing Time Chunking is success-rendering: 1. Capturing; getting all of your ideas, goals, and ambitions out of your head and on paper. Writing down goals and tasks helps to lay the foundation for execution. 2. Look for commonalities; Chunk those items on your capture list that correspond to the most common areas of life mastery: health, meaning & emotions, relationships, time, work/career/mission, finances, and spirituality. 3. The outcome; grouped with consistency success and happiness is the only outcome.

20. Develop A Sense Of Urgency.

"Highly productive people take the time to think, plan, and set priorities." These are the three essentials to why highly successful people mow through enormous amounts of work while others spend their time wastefully. You continuously tap away at your goals with a sense of urgency not to be confused with hastiness as that will result in accepting any and everything for a sense of gratification. Working continuously builds momentum, as you pedal a bike the first 10-20 feet are the hardest, gaining proper balance, getting the wheels to turnover, but after you continue to pedal you get to a point when the bike is riding with less and less effort and soon you get closer to your goal.

Contrary to common usage and interpretation, urgent does not mean fast or rush. Urgent does not mean being busy or being rushed or hurrying through things. Urgency is about opportunities and being an opportunist. Urgency is about being intentional and purposeful. Urgency is about priorities and preparedness. People with a strong sense of urgency to understand the value and beauty in each moment. This eliminates excuses because highly successful people know that they don't always have "tomorrow" or "I can do it later" "I can always get to it" because tomorrow isn't promised and most success-rendering moment might not exist the same day later. The very elite set dates and place time frames around everything that they do. This promotes integrity, growth, focus and respect to the said craft. Speed and quality is a duality that is rooted in study, research, intuition, and calculated risks.

21. Single Handle Every Task.

As we get excited about completing our desired goals, we begin to put on many hats. We try to complete too much at once. We sometimes can get over confident in the workload that we take on. It's not that we are not working hard enough or that we are not focused on our targets. Our adequacy, proficiency, creativeness suffer when we are involved in too much. A string of successes makes us think that we can actually take on more tasks. We must have self-control and stay consistent with what has rendered the most success. This is also rooted in not becoming content with superficial successes (over excited about the battle and war has not been won). We must isolate each task until completion without allowing them to wander onto other tasks for the feeling of gratification. Eat the Big ugly frog first there will be plenty of room for tadpoles.

Again I must give this entire ideology on "Eating the Big Ugly Frogs first" to Mr. Brian Tracy and his book "Eat that Frog." Mr. Tracy has gifted us with a great set of tools to aid us from Ants into butterflies. Get out of your own Way!

NOTE

NOTE

CHAPTER 4

If you take an L take two and make a W

If you take an L take two and make a W

As you experience transition from an ant to a butterfly, you must become comfortable while learning publicly. Integrity is who and what you do when no one is looking, but character is what you continuously present to the world over and over again, rather in the face of adversity or prosperity. This transitional period is character building. The beautiful thing is that you won't get it right every time. So the question is, "Why is this beautiful a thing?" It is beautiful because if you take an L, take two L's, you can make them into a W. As humans we are so bogged down by learning publicly. Learning publicly is also commonly known as failure. But failure has such a negative connotation and it is often hard for individuals, even if it makes sense or to wrap their heads around "failure" being a good thing. The word failure has been used so negatively that it's hard to see its light. What is that light you might ask? It is that small spectacle of energy off in far distance and its name is success. At the opposite end of failure is Success! "Every adversity, every failure, every heartache carries with it the seed for an equal or greater benefit." – Napoleon Hill. What we envision as being hard is that once we have failed or learned publicly, we think that learning publicly is rock bottom and there is no or very few ways to climb back out. We even believe that once climbing back out of a rut that we still must settle for just a slightly better derivative of the said failure. We are gifted with two things when we learn publicly and that is the first L, the loss, the defeat, the "Loss of Control." Now here is where the billionaires, the successors, the greats, and the leaders are made. Most will stop here and quit, while most say "I dOn'T qUiT." We can phrase it differently to practice insanity, or doing the same things over and over again expecting different results. What the "greats" do here is to take another L. You might think I'm the crazy one for telling you to take two L's as if one wasn't enough, but the second is the "Lesson"! Too many are idle in what has happened and now become victimized by the outcome. You become stuck! "Nothing happens to you everything happens because of you" George Cardone. Many of us hate this second L because one, it requires more work to be done and two because it's much easier to admit defeat, play the "I told ya/ told myself" card, point the finger and come up with inconceivable amounts of excuses and reasoning. While most dread this L, the greats embody this moment. "If you fail, do it fast." You want to learn publicly as quickly as you can, the longer you're idle in the moment the harder it will be to see the light at the end of the tunnel. The harder will it be to move and the easier will it be for negative emotions to set in, discourage and offset the momentum. Taking two L's is using the Power of Perspective to your advantage.

(Drawing of two hands making L's and a W)

Picture learning publicly like a car crash. BAM! The car is totaled, so we can go nowhere. Cars continue to pass by, some gawk but continue on their route. The car is completely banged up and capable of going nowhere. We can sit here moan, cry, kick the car, call it stupid, blame the other car, and allow any other reasoning to come in to play as to why we are now in this situation. Then comes creeping along, the Lesson. In this very moment you are at the highest capability to shape your reality into exactly that of which you so desire. What? Yes! A reference from the Paul's second epistle to the church of Corinth and he says in his 12th chapter verses 9-10 in reference to what Christ has told him:

"9 And He has said to me, 'My grace is sufficient for you, for power is perfected in weakness.' Most gladly, therefore, I will rather boast [a] about my weaknesses, so that the power of Christ may dwell in me. 10 Therefore I am well content with weaknesses, with [b]insults, with distresses, with persecutions, with difficulties, for Christ's sake; for when I am weak, then I am strong."

What Paul is saying here is, that when all is lost, when you have "done all you can," the car will never be driven again, that it is these precise moments that you are at your strongest! This is where the birth of resourcefulness, creativity, true optimism, craft fullness, persistence, and focus happens all at once! It is when we have lost it all, when we have learned publicly, and when nothing is adding up that we are literally gifted at this moment to transmute the desired into a reality! The car may have stopped, but you didn't. The destination is still ahead, we are gifted with a new approach, you'll "handle" things differently, and you'll plan differently. "I didn't fail 10,000 times I learned 10,000 ways my idea wouldn't work." Thomas Edison. You learn that if the car crash happened in causality to someone else that you must drive for the other person. In reality, this relates to having to plan in expectation where others will lack or what others will be unwilling to do. As well, never place the outcome of your reality into someone else hands.

What makes a true leader is their willingness to do more than they ask of others. If the car crash happened in causality to something you did or didn't do, you know you have a better understanding of how to navigate life. What I am describing here is that in life we will face L's, losses, setbacks, or born into poor circumstances. But, it's literally your perception, consciousness, and willingness to not accept that this is not the only possible outcome and that you have to remain in it; that will give you the power to change it. Two laws serve as knowledge and tools to grasping the concept of taking two L's.

The universe is made of 12 consistent laws, but there are two that are directly related to "taking 2 L's" and that is Law of Polarity and Law of Rhythm. I encourage you to read all of them as they are intertwined and related to one another; the conscious development of all leads to a marvelous reality.

What is Law of Polarity? Every thought (and therefore every intention) has two components—CONTENT and ENERGY. When you want to change something, the information is the content, while the energy supplied is the power that drives that intention. So, energy is intimately bound to the Law of polarity. Everything happens in two's (2), thus two direct opposites are really 2 inseparable parts of one thing! Hot and cold, left and right, up and down. Therefore, whatever you give energy to can manifest itself in the same way! Overflow is inseparable from lack, desiring affection is inseparable from being alone; EVERYTHING comes with potential for its opposite. Once you come into true understanding of this principle you are enlightened with its power. Self-awareness and clarity allows for this law to be maximized. With as much clarity as possible, write out what your desires are as well as their opposite and apply the Law of Polarity. Remember Content and Energy! In relation to taking two L's. Once you understand that opposites attract, Failure can instantly become Success, if you allow it!

Law of Rhythm. How many of us can dance? Well I suggest you learn and learn fast for your future's sake. At least get a 2-step.

Law of Rhythm is defined as: Everything vibrates and moves to certain rhythms. These rhythms establish seasons, cycles, stages of development, and patterns. Each cycle reflects the regularity of God's Universe. "Everything flows out and in; everything has its tides; all things rise and fall; the pendulum-swing manifests in everything; the measure of the swing to the right is the measure of the swing to the left; rhythm compensates."—The Kybalion. Very simply, Law of rhythm is that everything exist in a dance, ever-flowing, and everything is either growing or dying. We can easily see this law in our daily lives. In stocks there is always an up and down period; the seasons are one continuous flow from summer to winter, everything has a cycle, a pattern, thus a rhythm. Law of rhythm regulates our health, economy, relationships and spirituality. In light of taking 2 L's, we must understand very simply that everything has its season. Everything is always growing and dying. What the elites are able to do is that they see rhythm as a tool more than just something that forcibly governs their life. Instead, they are able to maximize each season. They are able to maximize the highs as well as the lows. They are able to gather composure when swaying left or right. The greats are able to rise above the "negative" parts of the cycle by never allowing the negative parts to shape their entire consciousness or focus. Control of one's emotions is the key here. Control your emotions. One must have complete control of their emotions to avoid being swayed from the right focus. What's interesting about understanding that everything has a cycle is that you are now gifted with super powers! Super powers? Yes you're a future-teller. Self-awareness of the season you're in enables you to maximize that season as well as prepare and shape yourself for the ever-consistent transition into the next season or level to follow. Why most get stuck in the first L is because they are still stuck in seasons that have been way over! Insanity, and doing the same things expecting different results. In terms of rhythm, insanity would be trying to plant during harvest season and trying to harvest during planting season. Being born and raised in Detroit, any Detroiter as well as many mid-westerners will attest that we could have all four seasons literally in one day! But one season that many dread is winter. When you were young, oh how you loved the snow, it meant no school for some days, snowball fights and snowmen, hot chocolate, and more. But as we got older, this blissfulness became more of a headache. Winter is gloomy, dark, lifeless, slower, cold, hazy, and feels unending. But winter has so many holidays we all love, and yes, hold that thought! Immediately, the dreadfulness sets in. For many will leave in the dark morning just to return at night. This season takes a toll on "some" of us. Many begin to wish for the warmer season or that the winter will just be mild and etc. But I had to realize that as much as I wanted it to be summer it just wasn't going to happen, and that I was only hindering the true benefits of this season! Yes, winter meant things were not growing, everything was slowed down, less outside activities, less interaction, and more consistent routines. But these were just some of the gifts! Things slowing down meant I was gifted with the ability to isolate and work on intricate areas that may not be permissible when the flow is ongoing. Less outside activities meant more time with self, more time for self-development, a period to literally create an entire new person. Less interaction meant more significant encounters, and time spent more wisely. Law of rhythm literally gifts you with the ability to Determine The Highs and Lows.

One thing that will be forever consistent is the cycle of high to low and vice versa. The great thing is that you decide the degree of each element. The level of intensity applied to either or results of the latter. If you maximize the lows or the down periods the higher are the highs and vice versa. Maximizing the high periods with regards that the lows must come allows for higher "low points." A low point for someone averagely living life might be missing a bill or etc. For us, our lows are realizing that we only have five buildings and we need to expand. The higher you are the higher are your lows! A "low" day for Warren Buffet is making only 3 million of the 5 million he wanted to make, a low "low" for many of us missing two-three meals! #MyLowsAreHigherThanYours. Hmm this takes the sting off the word low and you shape your mind to see the fruitfulness in every season, and the approach is not to think high versa low, but to become self-aware of every season as quick as possible to identify what actions that needs to be taken to maximize that season while in preparation to be positioned to maximize the one to follow. Taking two L's doesn't sound too bad after all.

IF YOU TAKE A L TAKE TWO AND MAKE A W

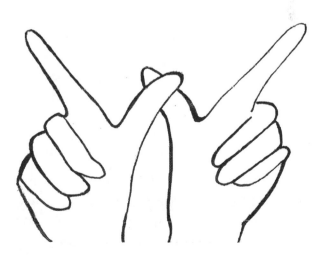

(PBnJ)

Perspective and Imagination

It's all about perspective, and what you allow the mind to create. Understanding the Power of Perception and Imagination is an imperative step to becoming a Conscious, Intentional, and a Purposeful Creator of Your Life! "Reality is what we take to be true. What we take to be true is what we believe. What we believe is based upon our perceptions. What we perceive depends on what we look for. What we look for depends on what we think. What we think depends on what we perceive. What we perceive determines what we believe. What we believe determines what we take to be true. What we take to be true is our reality."- pioneering physicist David Bohm. It's full circle and how we perceive the world becomes our reality. The degree at which you allow yourself to perceive, or your willingness to accept both seen and unseen and what that content is, becomes your reality. So, it becomes less of what is right versus wrong, but becoming subdued to the reality that whatever or wherever you apply the most energy or attention to will be produced. Therefore what you imagine it to be so is it. So a man thinketh, so he is…Uncertainty can be your greatest power or greatest restraint. It's your power to perceive, think, and thus create your own reality. Perception is often based on past events, so don't get to hating yourself because of it. Shifting one's perception to consistently generate authentic and pure desires isn't always easy as one may think. Here's where imagination completely takes it course. The "what if," the power of uncertainty. While past situations may cause you to perceive a current reality as impossible, pause! Here, you are gifted with the power of imagination and the power to think out a new reality with pure intent and the right amount of energy.

"Imagination is more important than knowledge. For knowledge is limited, whereas imagination embraces the entire world, stimulating progress, giving birth to evolution." – Albert Einstein. You "know" what has happened or what history says is supposed to happen. But now, you have the authority and power to create what can/could happen through perception and imagination. Imagination is the association of one's neural levels and physical expression. What you perceive + what-if = your outcome. "As an athlete, I have always used mental imagery, olfaction, and music to create not only a mood and mindset, but to alter my perceptions of the world around me. The smell of sunscreen and an upbeat pop-song always takes me away to a place of clear blue skies and bright sunshine even when the weather is dark, gray, and the world seems dreary…Encoding a perception that "Sweat Bliss" at a deep neural level allowed me to transcend through the physical discomfort as an Ironman triathlete and ultra-runner…The ability to use my imagination to reshape perceptions of reality allowed me to win races."-Christopher Bergland

Take Two L's: Perceive, Think, Create!

NOTE

NOTE

CHAPTER 5

The Art of Pure intentions and The Law of Attraction

The Art of Pure intentions and The Law of Attraction

E verything we do has a degree of intent. The content and intensity of this intent totally shapes our realities. Whatever you desire for your life, there is always an intention behind it. This intent decides the altitude of the outcome and if at all it happens, or how long it will be experienced. Pure intentions are rooted in knowing exactly what you want. Here is where most people start off wrong. Many will say I do not know what I want or it's too hard to foresee what the future truly holds for me. What the future truly holds is exactly what you intend for it to be. You must discover your "WHY.". Clarity on what you want to do, to be and etc. is the foundation to what will come to pass. Your intentions become pure when they are less about how others will perceive you, and when your desires are rooted in doing for others. This is not for reward, but because you are expressing the best version of yourself. That feeling of desire, or what you would do without being compensated for, is the roots to your pure intentions. Life is full of distractions. Oftentimes, we get caught up in what have become recycled displays of fame, success, and fortune that our desires and intent follow after these things. The thing about life is that we have the power to create the latter of the two. When we allow our intents to be based on that society we are living either in the past or in the moment, for the current state of society is what was done yesterday! My desires and intent are not to become as famous as or more famous than anyone, or to have more money than another because they have set the accumulation bar high.

However, my intentions become pure when I ask and press to have enough of everything I need to be the best version of myself, to facilitate the true good for the world and others around me. Love is foundational on two levels which defines the degree of your authenticity. To desire happiness for someone because you are doing it for them or only if you are a part of it is not true love. But to desire someone's well-being or happiness whether that involves you or not is true love. So, how do I have "pure" intentions? Pure intentions are the degree of authenticity. The more you press to become the best version of yourself the more pure your intent and actions are. This is why I fell in love with fitness. The reason I love fitness is because your best and most consistent results come from your desire to only please oneself. If you work out to be seen or only to please others you will always fall short.

Reason being why you have to fall in love with the betterment of yourself. Sure I can lose weight because my wife asked me to, but unless I wanted to lose that weight and saw how it would impact me then will I be enabled to benefit from this glorious experience. Another aspect of pure intentions is personality effect vs. character effect. We all have one or two great qualities that just come natural to us. An excerpt from another great book I suggest you read is "7 Habits of highly successful people." Here, the author speaks about the Inside-Out approach. That there must be Private Victories TM that precede Public Victories TM. The Inside-Out approach says that Private Victories TM precede Public Victories TM, and that making and keeping promises to ourselves precedes making and keeping promises to others. It says it is futile to put personality ahead of character, to try and improve relationships with others before improving ourselves. Inside-Out is a process — a continuing process of renewal, based on the natural laws that govern human growth and progress. It's an upward spiral of growth that leads to progressively higher forms of responsible independence and effective interdependence.

Our character, basically, is a composite of our habits. "Sow a thought, reap an action; sow an action, reap a habit; sow a habit, reap a character; sow a character, reap a destiny," the maxim goes…" "We are what we repeatedly do. Excellence, then, is not an act, but a habit."— Aristotle. So, I charge myself and you to play not on personality efforts because it leads to temporary success/rewards and superficial relationships, which causes deeper detriment for all involved. It is better to be true to thyself and waiver not for temporary pleasures or to please others because what is sowed will and always manifest. Give up your expectations of how people are supposed to react or respond and continue to be authentic in your ways and doings. People will always fall short of our expectations, but it is in our authenticity and purity of intent that we are protected from other shortcomings. In your meditation and/or prayer, ask to be:

- Positioned to receive exactly what you need.
- The peace and serenity that if it's meant to be it will be followed by the creativeness to create that which you are supposed to if the latter does not come to past.

Spend time deciding what your intentions are and always make sure what you have within you is pure while freeing yourself to align with that purity. Clarity, Clarity, Clarity. Do not deliver an unclear message to the universe or continue to align yourself with something that you're not or meant to be doing because you'll continue to receive unclear outcomes. Pure intentions are foundational, connected to, and dependent upon Law of Attraction all at the same time. Understanding pure intentions unlocks the true Power of Law of Attraction, but what is Law of Attraction.

The Power of the Law of Attraction. To simply define it: the Law of attraction is the ability to attract whatever you focus on into your life. Freebie: this law is unrestricted, meaning; regardless of age, ethnicity, nationality, beliefs; understanding and exercising its power, one can theoretically have whatever they so desire and wish for. I say theoretically because as many began to manifest this power it requires more and more focus as you progress in order not to become distracted, lose the intensity and thus fall back into the norm. All entertained thoughts become reality eventually. We are responsible for bringing both positive and negative influences into our lives. You have the freedom to take control of how your future develops, shaping it in the ways you choose. When you learn how to use the many powerful and practical tools associated with the Law of Attraction, you can start living and thinking in a more optimistic way that is specifically designed to attract even more euphoric events and positive experiences. The first step to understanding and mastering the law of attraction is controlling one's own thoughts. We must gain control of and understand the true nature of the thought that we entertain; and how that affects our future wellbeing. We often allow ourselves to entertain thoughts based on feelings; both good and bad. We also entertain thoughts so we can give more meaning to a situation, while this is a beautiful tool it is also a dangerous one as well. Dangerous because negative thoughts and feelings are always easier to entertain and thus produce themselves into our reality. Stress is dangerous not because stress is bad, but because there is good and bad stress and stress becomes dangerous because it's addictive. Your body can literally begin to crave negativity because one has allowed it to become its normative. With that being said, this is where the law of attraction becomes our greatest tool or our greatest enemy. "As a man thinketh so he is" ... "Watch your thoughts because they become your actions, actions become habits, habits become character, and character becomes destiny."

The law of attraction is only told when you dissect your thoughts and train yourself to only entertain the particular thoughts that permit and elicit the desired future. Training yourself on how to think and entertain your thoughts is the first step and it will progress you forward rather than keep you stagnant or pull you back. The second step is becoming a Visionary. I would like to give a shout out to my Alma Mater; Claflin University where our motto was "Be a Visionary Leader." Earlier in the book, we touched on power of foresight and the power of imagination. The successful, the great, the rich, whatever you would like to call them, all are great visionaries. They are able to see what others can't, or won't allow themselves to see. They aren't scared to allow themselves to see things from all perspectives even the ones that are unfamiliar or unpopular, for they know that today's reality does not set in stone what the future holds or could hold. One requirement I have before I call anyone my friend is that they must be able to do a handstand. Of course, I myself must be able to do the same. Now, for those who jumped to the physical handstands slow your roll, we're still mental. But let's look at the properties of a handstand. Upside-down (new perspective), Hand positioning (Balance), Different Muscles (Think differently), Takes more strength (More focus) and Change in blood flow (creativity). 1. New perspective; consistently allowing yourself to see things the best way that beget the best outcomes, notice I didn't say the most common or popular. 2. Balance; understanding the Law of rhythm, everything has a season and process, understanding when things are pulling one way that you have to sometimes go against the grain to regroup or flip things back around. 3. Think differently; "We cannot solve our problems at the same level of thinking that created them"- Albert Einstein. 4. More focus; you have to be willing to put more time in than anyone else, the more focus you have the less time it will take to understand, therefore, allowing for more time to learn more and continuously evolve into a better person! 5. Creativity; Innovation is the byproduct of creativity. There will be no reinventing the wheel, but creativity begets efficiency and proficiency, and it disables wastefulness. These are just a few qualities that permit a visionary mindset and as you dig deeper into foresight, imagination, and creativity, the world of tomorrow will become yours.

Rooted deeply in the Law of Attractions is Self-Worth and Internal Peace. If you can't control yourself how can you control others? Your actions are the outward expression of your inner voice. You are your inner voice. Because of this, it is life and death to your reality of knowing who you are and vibrating at ones highest frequency that then one may be enabled to control one's own destiny. Affirmations and Self Peace. Affirmations can enhance your use of the Law of Attraction by helping to totally reshape the core beliefs and assumptions that may be holding you back. They promote consistency, optimism and intense focus on the future you want to create. Both spoken and visual affirmations shape our today and tomorrow with consistency and faith. How you speak and think of yourself is what you will produce and ultimately what others will say and think about you as well. "Stick and stones may break my bones but words will never hurt" has to be the biggest myth in history. Words create languages and languages create communication avenues. So, the words you use to describe yourself are the reality that you allow yourself to receive! Affirmations are so powerful; at first it can seem difficult and even strange to say certain words about yourself because deep down you may not believe them. Stop! If you don't believe in yourself who will? This is where tenacity and power is created. Meditation is a great resource that many have found useful in creating a greater inner self. I quiet all the negative thoughts, I empty my mind of all "aint's" and "don't haves" I focus not on where I am but where I am going. Ultimately, I describe the person who I will become and not who I am today. This frees me from reflecting on past and current mishaps. This is daily that I have a set of affirmations I speak to myself and as I fully embody one, I add more. What this creates is an internal peace of self-worth. I am an Ant today, but now I walk and think as the butterfly I will become tomorrow! This permits the Law of Attraction to be at full power because all that I need to physically become a butterfly begins to come to me because of the way I think and thus now act.

(PBnJ) You can literally Think your desires into existence!

Useful tools: Affirmations, Vision boarding, Sticky Notes, Your circle of influence. As just previously described, I charge you to conduct a list of 10-20 sentence affirmations that you'll read every day when you first wake up and right before you go to sleep. This will become your inner voice in the face of adversity and in peace. We know that affirmations are key in the above mentioned because we know the law of polarity which can be exhibited by both. Next is I challenge you create a vision board. This can be as small as poster board or however large you decide to make it. I personally use three poster boards, and this allows me to have a kind of timeline of the year in thirds. The power behind vision boarding is that you will put the visual content of your goals that you will have to see every single day. Remember when we were younger and we would hang posts of cars or our favorite stars and be like "I'm going to drive that car one day or I'm going to be like her/him one day," statistic shows that kids who keep visual aids of their goals often achieve them faster and in greater quantity. Be a kid again! This will be one of your most powerful tools. On my vision board, I have quotes, cars, houses, and physical representations of my goals, just to name a few things. All have literally began to come to past. Sticky notes are a great tool as well in partner with vision boarding. Place sticky notes in strategic places so that even when life threats happens and we don't read our affirmations or don't look at vision board, as often as we need, they will become keen reminders of where we are and where we have to go! Some go overboard and stick note their entire house, but just a few that are strategically placed like in a rear view mirror, office desk, medicine cabinet, etc. are powerful. Last but certainly not least is your circle of influence! We all have friends, but they can be your greatest assets or greatest holdbacks. Do not confuse presence with support! Often we confuse people "sticking around" as support factors but they can be the very ones "praying for your downfall" –T Grizzley. If your friends are not motivating, kicking you in the butt and challenging you always to be or become your best self they are not friends or acquaintances. We often confuse emotions and feelings and allow toxic-ships to form. This is a tool that one must discover with personal efforts. You have to really dissect how a person has influenced your ideas. A simple "haha you could never do that" seems so friendly, but when you reflect "hmm I really stop pursuing that thing" you realize that it's the simple things which are said and done that actually make true friends. I can honestly say the people I have labeled friends all encourage, motivate, challenge, and push me to be the best I can ever think to be. While acquaintances and family say "that'll never work or that will be a lot work or that's impossible" my friends say "well if you think you can do it, do it, you have my support, how can I help, ooh I know someone with similar ideas." I ask you to dissect and decipher all your –ships, boyfriends/girlfriends, best-friends, friends, and other deemed important –ships in life. You will either develop a new circle of influence or redistribute the amount of influence these individuals have on your life.

NOTE

NOTE

CHAPTER 6

Isolation is Ok: A seed requires darkness to grow

Isolation is Ok: A seed requires darkness to grow

L
ike a seed starts germinating from underground, so do we as ants before we evolve into the beautiful butterflies of tomorrow. The period of isolation can be a challenging one, but only the one that yields the greatest benefits if you allow it. Before a seed becomes a flower, and then thus a tree; a seed must be planted into the ground and covered. It is in this darkness that a seed first relies on itself before it can affect its environment. A seed, as it germinates uses "food" stored within itself before it fully germinates and sprouts, thereby, permitting photosynthesis or the use of carbon dioxide and release of oxygen back into the earth; as it pertains to us affecting the world around you. Very interesting to know that in order to grow, a seed must rely on itself first. That it has to push through what is on top of it in order to flourish. Isolation has had a negative connotation, much like failure, because it has been used as a form of punishment. "Go to your room, sit in the dark" "sit by yourself," even prisoners are isolated from others as punishment. What's interesting that isolation has been such a successful punishment tool, and continues to plague great personalities from ever reaching their full potential because they see not the period of isolation as a great reward. Isolation and solidarity has proven to change people, make them go crazy, insane, they often leave isolation fatigued, weak, changed and not for the better. But throughout history there have been countless representation of those who did not allow isolation to be a punishment, but as a tool to become better. Nelson Mandela spent 27 years in prison, but it was in isolation and the battle within himself did he first conquer that enabled him to affect the world around. As we touched on earlier; let go of fear! What are you afraid of? The reason most people resist and fight isolation or the period to be alone is because they have fear of themselves. Many are scared to face the truth of themselves. Jack Fong, a sociologist at California State Polytechnic University who has studied solitude. "When you have these moments, don't fight it. Accept it for what it

is. Let it emerge calmly and truthfully and don't resist it, "Your alone time should not be something that you're afraid of." "It's a deeper internal process," notes Matthew Bowker, a psychoanalytic political theorist at Medaille College who has researched solitude. Productive solitude requires internal exploration, a kind of labor which can be uncomfortable, and even excruciating. Yes, it is hard at first but do trust that it will turn into the most rewarding experience. There is no greater relationship than the one you have with yourself!

You should have an ever craving desire to dissect and discover your inner self. Many greats often reflect on; "if I spent more time working on myself how I could've done more for the people they were trying to do more for!" Isolation is where you discover exactly who you are and what you can be. We all have versions of ourselves that are ugly, difficult to face, we hate to revisit moments of weakness and etc. But this isolation is judgment free and permits us to evolve. Very early on I said I had to find all the Xavier's that were the traffic on my road to all hopes and dreams. This period can be so excruciating, you want to cry out for help while simultaneously keeping a guard up and not letting anyone in. I charge you to let yourself in! We have become such a group oriented society that we can no longer think for ourselves without the backing of others, social medias have us all connected all the time that solitary has become devalued that it's almost sinister to be alone. Bowker says. "Put another way, a person who can find a rich self-experience in a solitary state, is far less likely to feel lonely when alone." It is in isolation that we become more in tune with ourselves that we may be permitted to greater interact with the world around us. The power of isolation comes with the realization that if anyone wishes to do anything great you will enter a period where you are on the island by yourself. There will always be moments where one must rely on oneself to carry-on. If you do not know yourself, how can you then fully conquer anything beyond yourself? As stated earlier, Private Victories TM beget Public Victories TM. "When people take these moments to explore their solitude, not only will they be forced to confront who they are, they just might learn a little bit about how to out-maneuver some of the toxicity that surrounds them in a social setting." – Fong. It's in isolation that we regain power of the outside world. Everything slows down, we are able to dissect everything in pieces, and this allows us to reconnect with our true selves and maneuver the best way forward. Read this next quote a few times, as if you are not willing to sacrifice all that is asked in order to be elicited your desired future to save yourself from downfall now.

"If you're going to try, go all the way. Otherwise, don't even start. This could mean losing girlfriends, wives, relatives and maybe even your mind. It could mean not eating for three or four days. It could mean freezing on a park bench. It could mean jail. It could mean derision. It could mean mockery—isolation. Isolation is the gift. All the others are a test of your endurance, of how much you really want to do it."
— Charles Bukowski, Factotum

(PBnJ) You Control The Isolation!

Again, contrary to belief, isolation is a beautiful tool and technique. Guess what, it doesn't have to be some drawn out thing! You don't have to book a trip to no-man's land for three months to be renewed. Again, life is so much simpler. Isolation is most powerful when it is intent, purposeful and has boundaries. I Challenge you to the 30/30/30 Challenge. 30 minutes away from social media (A time where you would normally be permitted to use social media, so work related doesn't count); 30 minutes outside with no music, no phones, no talking; 30 minutes of meditation where you sit in a quiet space and focus on your inner self. I challenge you do this consistently as possible for 30 days and notice how more incline you are with yourself and the outside world. I encourage you research meditation techniques, discover what works best for you! Meditation and these strategic breaks from social media has become one of my greatest strengths. I don't feel pressured to know what anyone else is doing or thinking or valued by amount of likes and comments, but it allows me to find confidence in content. If 30 minutes is too much, you can start with 15. But I challenge you make it intent and purposeful, challenge yourself with a goal each time you are on isolation. A common goal of mine is to reassure my self-confidence. I often use large portions of my isolation time to charge myself with affirmations that realign me with pure intentions and the ability to trust myself. We have become pressured as a society to always be connected and stay up to date. Becoming confident in being alone and strategically using isolation/mediation is the beginning stages of our cocoon. We are slowly evolving from ants to butterflies. If you are afraid or do not understand the power of meditation/ isolation, you will prematurely erupt from your cocoon and be unprepared to flourish as the beautiful butterfly you are meant to be.

The Power of Meditation and Isolation of the Mind

There are different ways to meditate, these are focused-attention, or mind meditation. You focus on one specific thing like breathing, a sensation in your body or a particular object outside of you. Meditation and isolation of mind is one of man's most powerful tools in achieving his/her goals. Earlier, we touched on the power of our thoughts and literally thinking our desired realities into existence, and that so a man thinks so is he. But, meditation and isolating the mind is twofold. It's the ability to isolate and focus on one thing, until that thing manifest itself in the way of your desires. As well, meditation is being able to separate oneself from everything and allowing everything to happen without reacting. This separation is until you have developed into the person most readily to positively affect your reality and render the desired goals for your future self. Meditation is the ability to hone in on one thing until it's pleasingly fruitful or hone in oneself until you are pleasingly fruitful to your dreams and goals. Meditation allows you to silence all noise around that very thing or yourself until what is most needed is attracted to it or you. Meditation stills everything! It intricately and calmingly realigns everything until elevation is rendered to you. Isolating the mind to that of a goal, and only that goal zeros out and eliminates anything that is not attributing to its manifestation. When you push to allow your mind to completely engulf the reality of that goal, you not only get the goal but the steps as well. You are gifted with a conscious road map, intuition and "favor" that ever align you with the goal. Isolating yourself allows for you to see all the versions of yourself, both good and bad, allowing you to see the habits that are enabling the reality of your goals or hindering them. Meditation gives you a self-check menu to see habits, actions, priorities, focuses, recreations that are positively affecting the fruition of your dreams and goals. Meditation allows you to calm the pressures of anxiety, anger, confusion, and is unlimited to the fixation of many undesired issues (physical & mental). Meditation enables the mind and body to be at the best vibrance or best presentation of self. Meditation gives you total control over your present reality as well as your future reality. It's when the mind is isolated that we are gifted with the exact creativity to create the reality we're focused on rather it be for that one thing or yourself.

Meditation allows you to render whatever reality you focus on even over pain, sickness, setbacks, misconceptions, missed marks, and etc. I encourage you to research more on meditation and what practices are best for you. It's in meditation that we are affirming our affirmations where our mind escapes to that reality. 5 things Meditation enables:

1. Zooming In

Being able to see the intricacies that must be adjusted or become habitual to be ever success rendering. The little things.

2. Zooming Out

Being able to see everything at once. Able to see what is working in congruence, and what is working in hindrance. Able to see what major moves must be taken in order to be in alignment.

3. Pausing

You're enabled to slow everything down and this gives you the ability to think and readjust to better effect rendered outcomes.

4. Changing

Being able to make the necessary changes; rather they be cutting or adding habits or increasing the frequency or decreasing frequency of habits.

5. New Reality

In whatever outcomes your meditation yields you are gifted a new reality. A reality that is fully aligned with the yielding of your goals and dreams.

NOTE

NOTE

CHAPTER 7

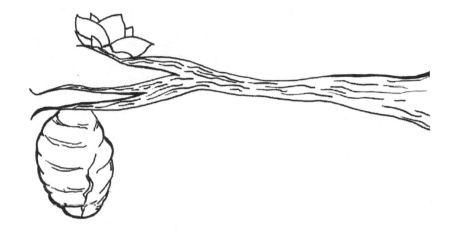

Are you ok with tomorrow: The Cocoon

Are you ok with tomorrow: The Cocoon

A s much as we may think we are ready, we must first conquer today before we can be able to control tomorrow. Some of you may be like me, riled up and ready to go, but we're still ants. Like me, you have read or will read similar books filled with more countless gems for advancement, and you will be ready to implement everything; wake up tomorrow exactly where you want to be! Okay, open your eyes, we are still ants in this very moment. This isn't what the cocoon is all about, rather it's the beginning of actions toward your new desired future. The cocoon is the period of habit, consistency, and persistence. Take for example working out; just because you learn how to use every machine in the gym does not mean: (a) you suddenly become the world strongest woman/man ((b) every machine will be useful to your desired goals (c) you have identified and mastered the sequence in which the what machines should be used to push you to your so desired goals. Like we all have different body types, and at a vast difference of stages in our lives; our utilization of these machines will vary greatly. The machines in reference are the plethora of success rendering knowledge or the practices we long to identify and learn. But as we learn while we are still young, what works for one person doesn't mean it will work for another. Everything that glitters isn't gold; what might seem like the perfect schedule, the step-by-step success formula, if it doesn't work for you it becomes a hindrance! As to the much reason you decided to read this book to discover how to evolve from an ant into a butterfly, it is worthy to note that it isn't something that happens overnight. The cocoon is first discovering through all the scholarly articles, self-help books, motivational seminars, focus groups, step-by-step success planners, etc. what formula that advances you! This is where you become a creature of habit, consistency, and persistence. Once I am aware of what permitted success and advancement, then come repetition and habit: doing it as often as needed, consistency: doing it "how" and "when" it was most beneficial, and persistence: in the face of adversity or hindrance, still accomplishing and surpassing the goal. The cocoon is challenging, putting all this knowledge together, and identifying what does and what doesn't work. This is why many avoid or try to go around the cocoon because too many are in a rush. Are you okay with tomorrow? You must have an ever-longing passion for growth. Get rich quick schemes never work, quick gratifications always lead to long periods of downfall. A fruit that is bore in hours will lack the potency, nutritional content, and wholesomeness of a fruit that took weeks to bore! Embrace the process! Accepting there is always room for improvement, that yesterday's victories are not tomorrow guarantees but that today's habits are their securities. Understanding, enjoying and looking for periods to cocoon will keep one above the rest. In reference to failure, we have already redefined it but in terms of accepting tomorrow, Will Smith puts it great and gives a clearer picture. "Fail early, fail often, fail forward...Seek failure...When you go to the gym and work out you are seeking failure. You seek to take your muscles to failure because that is where the adaptation and growth is...Successful people fail as often as possible...live at the edge of your capability, live at the point where you almost fall....failure permits evolution!" This is the cocoon, you are seeking all the areas where you will most definitely fail. This is the period you do everything a butterfly would do even though you're an ant. You tirelessly become habitual, consistent, and persistence in identifying every area that is hindering you from your desired future. Consistently place yourself at the point of limitation in each of these areas to which you are guaranteed to fail; that's when you force yourself to grow! "In order to reach new height a plane first experience turbulence!"-Xavier Robertson. This is when everything comes to you and before you know it where you've had hands you sprouted wings! Fall in love with "not being where you desire to be," but be filled with confidence that you are doing what it takes now to get there. With this mindset the fruition of your dreams will begin to happen faster and faster. You'll be cocooning and evolving into a better you overnight, every week, or as needed to be exactly where you desire. Embrace today, that you are gifted with everything that you need to control tomorrow; that even if you fall short you are still infinite miles from where you were. It doesn't get easier, instead you get stronger, smarter, and more focused. "Yesterday is but today's memory, and tomorrow is today's dream." Khalil Gibran. I'm in love with, "even if my efforts of yesterday do yield my desired outcome for today, my efforts were not in vain and as always I'm the captain of my ship." "Self-discipline is an act of cultivation. It requires you to connect today's actions to tomorrow's results. There's a season for sowing a season for reaping. Self-discipline helps you know which is which." Gary Ryan Blair. It is this period that will yield your desires. Can you remain self-disciplined, utilize what is most useful from this book as well as others. Can you twirl that silk and cocoon time after time no matter how long or how intense it will be to become the butterfly you desire and the world deserves? I touched on this earlier, so lose your emotions. We often allow fatigue, being tired, or the feeling of having "done a lot, or all we can" to be a marker of when enough is enough. Remember, as a man thinketh so he is, so until you have what you desire you are not doing what is necessary or doing enough of what is necessary or identifying the most opportune timing! Simple. "When I was young, I observed that nine out of ten things I did were failures. So, I did ten times more work."– George Bernard Shaw...Here we become relentless. After all, an ant isn't meant to become a butterfly. But we learned earlier "what was" only gives us the tools to shape what will be. So what others think, what the current world says, what is or isn't, or what has happened is irrelevant when you do what has to be done, when it needs to be done, again and again to produce the fruits of that labor. Our concern isn't that an ant biologically doesn't evolve into a butterfly, but that of our willingness to do what it takes, time after time to achieve greater results. Are we willing to place ourselves in situations when all the numbers and the odds say no, and evolve into what exactly we have or need to be in those very moments? When any opportunity presents itself, we flourish as if it had been written into the plans all along.

NOTE

NOTE

CHAPTER 8

Be the Butterfly

Be the Butterfly

Being Comfortable with being Uncomfortable *"How does one become a butterfly?" Pooh asked pensively.*

'You must want to fly so much that you are willing to give up being a caterpillar (ant; for our sake),' Piglet replied.

'You mean to die?' asked Pooh.

'Yes and no,' he answered. 'What looks like you will die, really you will live on."

Throughout the entirety of this book, I have been challenging you to do one thing: "Rid yourself of your comfort zone." Again, "We cannot solve our problems at the same level of thinking that created them"- Albert Einstein. We cannot expect to advance in life at the same comfort zone we begin at. This is true as well if we desire to have continuous amount of advancement and success in life. What remains true about the future is that it is unfamiliar, and so we must be willing to subdue what is uncommon and unfamiliar to the present and past! The comfort of an Ant is dark and underground while the comfort of a butterfly is the wind flowing beneath its wings as the sun glistens, as it's drawn into the sweet aroma of a flower. These are two drastically different comforts. Not until you are willing to rid the comfort of your current reality, you will not allow yourself to reap the reality you so much desire. We must rid ourselves to what was comfortable as an ant in order to be rewarded with the comforts of a butterfly. Where we hang out and spend our time, we don't see butterflies climbing in and out of holes in the ground. Your comfort zone is a magnetic field that attracts what will be present in your future. Where are you comfortable? Who are you comfortable around? Where are you comfortable socializing. Where are you comfortable being seen at? Who are you comfortable being seen and interacting with? Adjusting your comfort zone to that of the reality of dreams and desires allows you to reap that outcome. It's not comfortable socializing with doctors when you are just a sophomore biology student, but when you're able to press pass uncomfortableness, you are enabled to get to where you want to be. But because we are comfortable being uncomfortable, we took a seat instead of running away. You decided to question where you didn't understand, instead of becoming discouraged that you were presently ignorant about the topic, being comfortable with being uncomfortable allows you to go farther in shorter intervals of time. So, while you are still a sophomore, it is your willingness to press pass your social comfort where you are rewarded with countless favor (network, broaden vernacular, advantage to opportunities, etc.). This is just a vague example but it's the degree and intensity of your comfort level that will decide if and ever your dreams and desires come to fruition. Remember this is your story, leave the feelings and emotions at the door, and if you want it, then NO is never an option.

Get out of your own way! Rid your comfort zone.

Make friends out of your comfort zone.

Find people who are where you want to be or as well traveling to the same destination. Remember our circle of influence is the key. Here you could find your mentor as well.

Put yourself in uncomfortable environments.

Go to networking events, expos, meet-ups etc. that are focalized on your goals. Attend more workshops, gatherings, seminars etc. that are discussing and educating about things that pertain to your dreams and goals.

Seek and don't fight discomfort.

Don't be hesitant to be uncomfortable and do not fight it when it happens. Instead allow yourself to be positively molded and be pushed to evolving toward what is needed to advance you to your dreams and goals.

Remember, you will always hit exactly what you're aiming for!

Key Wrap-Up

PBnJ: The world's greatest Sandwich! Whether you agree or not it still is. But the PB&J's are key takeaways from the various topics we discussed as we journey from Ants into Butterflies. This key Warp Up is to be taken as the "quick-go-to" as PB&J's have always, till this day, been my go-to sandwich to solve any amount of hunger, it's fitting that these PB&J's be taken in light needing quick direction.

Find The Ugly.

Be Ant Now (Maximizing Your Present Season).

Eat The Big Ugly Frogs First.

If you take an L take two and make a W.

Tap into who you are so you can create what it is you want to become; Law of Attraction and Pure Intentions.

Isolation is Ok: A seed requires darkness to grow.

Tomorrow is Ok.

Be the Butterfly.

(PBnJ) Power of great Mentor

A great mentor is one of the greatest assets you can have on your journey to success. There is no greater influencer or combination than an individual that has lived, wants to be an open book to you and desires to see you succeed in life farther than them. If you're lucky (humble and focused), you will have multiple as well as some will choose you! These are my 5 qualities of a great Mentor and what you should look for before becoming someone's' Mentee: 1. "Mentors are free." If anyone is requiring you to pay to gain knowledge from them, they desire only to make you as good as what you can afford. Mentors are free which is why they are who they are, and what they can provide is so invaluable. 2. "Mentors desire to mature you both personally and professionally." A great Mentor understands the balance of personal and professional life and desires to make sure you are attending to both, they are able to identify weak areas you yourself cannot see and will challenge you to ever evolve into a better personality with high level of achievement. 3. "A Mentor reestablishes your hope and will not bite their tongue to professionally tell you to "get your stuff together." A great Mentor will be able to identify when you are acting within your highest self -worth. This will be to give hope and reestablish your confidence when faced with adversity. When acting in negligence that renders you out of character acts, they will not bite their tongue in a corrective nature rather, they will talk you out of your state of negligence. In both they know how to reaffirm who you are and where you're going to. 4. "A Mentor is a great source of network." A mentor should be able to facilitate viable networking opportunities that would help you in attaining your goals. A great Mentor when they cannot deliver, they know someone who can and can open doors that you yourself cannot open. 5. "Mentors are transparent." A great mentor desires not to show all of their accolades, but all their flaws and shortcomings as well. A great Mentor does this so you have a true depiction of success and enabled to repeat where they excelled and avoid where they fell.

(PBnJ) Keep the squares out of the circle!

It is imperative for the future you so desire and are destined for that you choose your cycle carefully. I'll say this a few ways: associating with different minded/focused individuals will divert you from your goals; vibing with the wrong energies will drain yours; true friends challenge the process of an idea not the idea itself; your circle should have challenging presence of a "better" and to not keep another down, but rather be a motivator; the wrong individuals close to you can be the very cancers to your dreams if you are not mindful of them; and etc.

Your circle should elevate you. Your close associates (friends, homies, girls, bros, besties, partners, team mates, etc) should

Have like-mindedness of overall wellness of the entirety of the group.

Have like-mindedness of desired successful future.

Challenge you to be the best version of you at all times.

Challenge you to evolve into a better being.

Promote and praise your good qualities and give constructive criticism to areas you could improve.

Conscious of how you all complement each other's lives and maximize that very aspect and divert to nothing else.

#Squad

(PbnJ) Social Perception.

How were and are you being socially perceived. This is a good measurement of who you think you are and what others actually view you as. This helps one avoid a plethora of misconceptions, unwarranted situations, gives insights on what to do and a clear understanding of where you stand within your reality. For many, we think we have attained these roles or are on track to become a particular piece to a puzzle. Whether this "derived attainment" is in someone life or business, we are shocked by the outcome when our desires do not match our reality. In the midst of "jealousy and hate" (criticism) we find these beautiful jewels for advancement. It's only partly true that "what others say does not matter" as constructive criticism or hate, both provide a clear indication of where you are. Social perception is a great tool, but too often many get caught in what is being said or done (or not done) and fail to realize the benefit of what has happened. The world has a way of letting you know very abrasively whether you are on track or not.

Adhering to these notions correctly allots for advancement rather than destruction. Let's look at the enormous amount of negativity social perception has been undergone by one particular group for a very long time. This particular group is still fighting to be equal in the eyes of their opposite. Social perception if used properly becomes like a map in how to guide oneself from an ant to a butterfly. This particular group is Women. For centuries, they have been deemed inadequate both intellectually and physically to man. This social perception discouraged millions and millions from their true potential, but for many more millions this gave them a direct understanding of where "they are not" and where they had to go. In a nutshell, people will always have something to say (social perception) and if you only listen to the words which they uttered, prepare to be lost forever but break down what is being said into bits and if any inkling has any application to you, they have just given you a free insight on where you can become better! #LeaveTheEmotionsAtTheDoor

(PBnJ) Perspective and Imagination.

It's all about perspective and what you allow the mind to create. We briefly touched on this earlier. Understanding the Power of Perception and Imagination is an imperative step to becoming a Conscious, Intentional, and Purposeful Creator of Your Life! "Reality is what we take to be true. What we take to be true is what we believe. What we believe is based upon our perceptions. What we perceive depends on what we look for. What we look for depends on what we think. What we think depends on what we perceive. What we perceive determines what we believe. What we believe determines what we take to be true. What we take to be true is our reality."- pioneering physicist, David Bohm. It's a full circle how we perceive that the world becomes our reality. The degree at which you allow yourself to perceive, or your willingness to accept both seen and unseen and what that content is, becomes your reality. So it becomes less of what is right versus wrong, but becoming subdued to the reality that whatever you apply the most energy or attention to will be produced. Therefore what you imagine it to be so is it. So as a man thinketh so he is…Uncertainty can be your greatest power or greatest restraint. It's your power to perceive, think, and thus create your reality. Perception is often based on past events, so don't get to hating yourself because of it. Shifting one's perception to consistently generate authentic and pure desires isn't always easy. Here's where imagination takes it course. The "what if," the power of uncertainty. While past situations may cause you to perceive a current reality, impossible, pause! Here you are gifted with the power of imagination, and the power to think a new reality with pure intent and the right amount of energy.

"Imagination is more important than knowledge. For knowledge is limited, whereas imagination embraces the entire world, stimulating progress, giving birth to evolution." – Albert Einstein.

You "know" what has happened or what history says is supposed to happen. But now you have the authority and power to create what can/ could happen through perception and imagination.

Imagination is the association of one's neural levels and physical expression. What you perceive + what-if = your outcome. "As an athlete, I have always used mental imagery, olfaction, and music to create not only a mood and mindset, but to totally alter my perceptions of the world around me. The smell of sunscreen and an upbeat pop-song always takes me away to a place of clear blue skies and bright sunshine even when the weather is dark, gray, and the world seems dreary…Encoding a perception that "Sweat = Bliss" at a deep neural level allowed me to transcend physical discomfort as an Ironman triathlete and ultra-runner…The ability to use my imagination to reshape perceptions of reality allowed me to win races."- Christopher Bergland.

Take Two L's: Perceive, Think, Create!

(PBnJ) You can literally Think your desires into existence!

Useful tools: Affirmations, Vision boarding, Sticky Notes, Your circle of influence. As just previously described, I charge you conduct a list of 10-20 one sentence length affirmations that you'll read every day when you first wake up and right before you go to sleep. This will become your inner voice in the face of adversity and in peace. We know that affirmations are keys in both because we know the law of polarity. Next is I challenge you create a vision board. This can be as small as poster board or however large you decide to make it. I personally use three poster boards, and this allows me to have a kind of a timeline of the year in thirds. The power behind vision boarding is that you will put visual content of your goals that you will have to see every single day. Remember when we were younger and we would hang posts of cars or our favorite stars and be like "I'm going to drive that car one day or I'm going to be like her/him one day," statistic shows that kids who keep visual aids of their goals often achieve them faster and in greater quantity. Be a kid again! This will be one of your most powerful tools. On my vision board, I have quotes, cars, houses, and physical representations of my goals, just to name a few things. All have literally began to come to past. Sticky notes are a great tool as well in partner with vision boarding. Place sticky notes in strategic places so that even when "life happens" and we don't read our affirmations or don't look at vision board, as often as we need, they will become keen reminders of where we are and where we have to go! Some go overboard and sticky note their entire house, but just a few that are strategically placed like in a rear view mirror, office desk, medicine cabinet, etc. are powerful. Last but certainly not least is your circle of influence! We all have friends, but they can be your greatest assets or greatest holdbacks. Do not confuse presence with support! Often we confuse people "sticking around" as support factors, but they can be the very ones "praying on your downfall" –T Grizzley. If your friends are not motivating, kicking you in the butt and challenging you always to be or become your best self they are not friends or acquaintances. We often confuse emotions and feelings and allow toxic-ships to form. This is a tool that one must discover with personal efforts. You have to really dissect how a person has influenced your ideas. A simple "haha you could never do that" seems so friendly but when you reflect "hmm I really stop pursuing that thing" you realize that it's the simple things that are said and done that actually make true friends. I can honestly say the people I have labeled friends all encourage, motivate, challenge, and push me to be the best I can ever think to be. While acquaintances and family say "that'll never work or that will be a lot of work or that's impossible" my friends say "well if you think you can do it, do it, you have my support, how can I help, ooh I know someone with similar ideas." I ask you to dissect and decipher all your –ships, boyfriends/girlfriends, best-friends, friends, and other deemed important –ships in life. You will either develop a new circle of influence or redistribute the amount of influence these individuals have on your life.

(PBnJ) You Control The Isolation!

Again, contrary to belief, isolation is a beautiful tool and technique. Guess what, it doesn't have to be some drawn out thing! You don't have to book a trip to no-man's land for three months to be renewed. Again, life is so much simpler. Isolation is most powerful when it is intentful, purposeful, and has set boundaries. I challenge you to the 30/30/30 Challenge. 30 minutes away from social media (A time where you would normally be permitted to use social media, so work or related doesn't count); 30 minutes outside with no music, no phones, no talking; 30 minutes of meditation where you sit in a quiet space and focus on your inner self. I challenge you to do this consistently as possible for 30 days and notice how more incline you are with yourself and the outside world. I encourage you research meditation techniques, discover what works best for you! Meditation and these strategic breaks from social media has become one of my greatest strengths. I don't feel pressured to know what anyone else is doing or thinking or valued by amount of likes and comments, but it allows me to find confidence in content. If 30 minutes is too much, you can start with 15. But I challenge you make it intentful and purposeful, challenge yourself with a goal each time you are in isolation. A common goal of mine is to reassure my self-confidence. I often use large portions of my isolation time to charge myself with affirmations that realign me with pure intentions and the ability to trust myself. We have become pressured as a society to always be connected and to stay up to date. Becoming confident in being alone and strategically using isolation/mediation is the beginning stages of our cocoon. We are slowly evolving from ants to butterflies. If you are afraid or do not understand the power of meditation/isolation, you will prematurely erupt from your cocoon and be unprepared to flourish as the beautiful butterfly you are meant to be.

The Power of Meditation and Isolation of the Mind

There are different ways to meditate, these are focused-attention, or mind meditation. You focus on one specific thing like breathing, a sensation in your body or a particular object outside of you. Meditation and isolation of mind is one of man's most powerful tools in achieving his/her goals. We touched on the power of our thoughts and literally thinking your reality into existence, and that so a man thinks so is he. But meditation and isolating the mind is twofold. It's the ability to isolate and focus on one thing, until that thing manifest itself in the way of your desires. As well, meditation is being able to separate oneself from everything and allowing everything to happen without reacting. Separate yourself until you have developed into the person most readily to positively affect your reality and render the desired goals for your future self. Meditation is the ability to hone in on one thing until it's pleasingly fruitful or hone in oneself until you are pleasingly fruitful to dreams and goals. Meditation allows you to silence all the noise around that very thing or yourself until what is most needed is attracted to it or you. Meditation stills everything's! While it intricately, calmingly realigns everything until elevation is rendered to you. Isolating the mind to that of a goal, and only that of the goal zeros out and eliminates anything that is not attributing to its manifestation. When you push to allow your mind to completely engulf the reality of that goal, you not only get the goal but the steps as well. You are gifted with a conscious road map and intuition and the "favor" that ever aligns you with the goal of the intensity of the focus is kept. Isolating yourself allows for you to see all the versions of yourself, good and bad, allowing you to see habits that are enabling the reality of your goals or hindering them. Meditation gives you a self-check menu to see habits, actions, priorities, focuses, recreations that are positively affecting the fruition of your dreams and goals. Meditation allows you to calm the pressures of anxiety, anger, confusion, and is unlimited to the fixation of many undesired issues (physical & mental). Meditation enables the mind and body to be at the best vibrancy or best presentation of self. Meditation gives you control over your present reality as well as your future reality. It's when the mind is isolated that we are gifted with the exact creativity to create the reality we're focused on rather it is for that one thing or yourself.

I and AM are two of the most powerful words that exist in the English language. As, whatever is placed after them shapes your reality! List out (9) I Am statements and repeat these daily:

1. _____

2. _____

3. _____

4. _____

5. _____

6. _____

7. _____

8. _____

NOTE

NOTE

About the Author

Xavier "Mr. Hope" Robertson born and raised on the westside of Detroit. I attended one of the most prestigious high schools in Detroit, Renaissance High School. Continuing, went on to complete his Bachelors of Science in Biology and become a Visionary Leader from Claflin University, CU. Since graduation, I've had multiple successful businesses, and now currently an Author, Life Coach, Music Manager, Motivational Speaker, Philanthropist and Serial Entrepreneur. Driven by facilitating success, wealth and betterment for others; My primary goal is for all to see and fulfill their highest potential by unlocking your success mindset!

I am HOPE. I believe we have lost hope in our capabilities as a people. Some honestly believe that where they start they aren't meant to go much further from there. Some strive to go further and are immediately hit with LIFE. Everything is so readily available yet so un-accessible. The most educated generations, the most advanced, yet mentally, physically, and financially so many are losing. So man thinketh ! SO a man believeth, So a man becomes habitual . will the results reflect it!. I am here to restore hope in our capabilities within ourselves, with our families, within our communities to establish a continuum of HEALTH WEALTH and FREEDOM for generations and generations to come. It's not hard work we have to do its consistency!

Visit Mrhopemotivates.com

Mr. Hope Motivates is here restore hope in our capabilities within ourselves, with our families, within our communities to establish a continuum of Health Wealth and Freedom for generations and generations to come. It's not hard work we have to do its consistency! Visit to book Mr. Hope for Motivational Speaking (seminars, panels, school events, etc), Mentoring, Coaching, and Consulting. Visit for Mr. Hope apparel!

Printed in the United States
By Bookmasters